Business Guide to

Saudi Arabia

Longman ⸬   WORLD OF INFORMATION

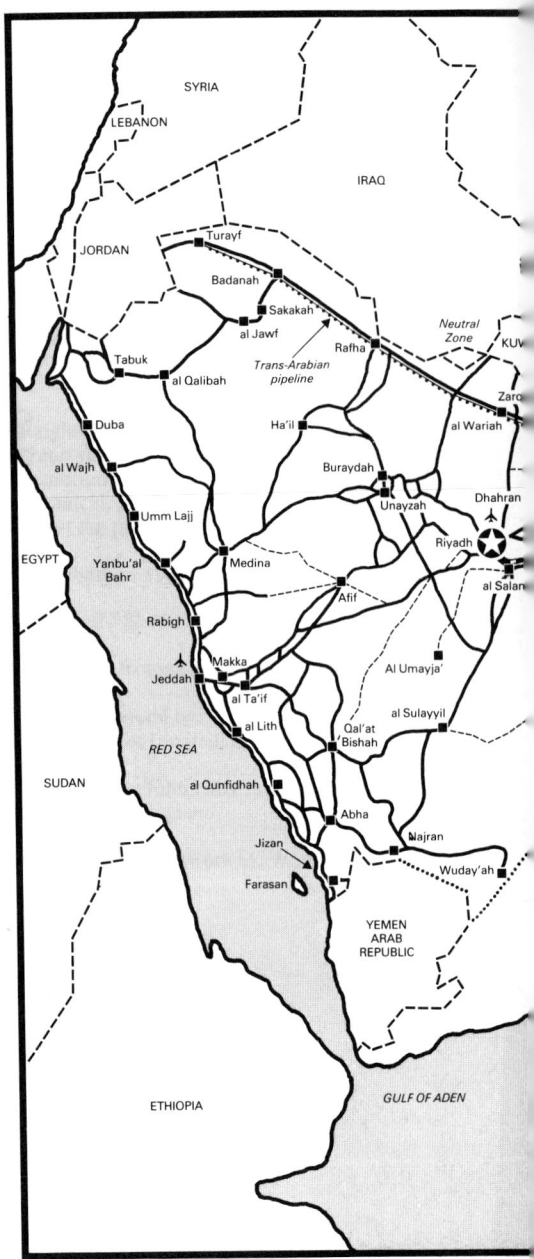

SYRIA

LEBANON

IRAQ

JORDAN

Turayf

Badanah

Sakakah

al Jawf

Neutral Zone

KUW

Tabuk

al Qalibah

Rafha

Trans-Arabian pipeline

Zaro

al Wariah

Duba

Ha'il

al Wajh

Buraydah

Unayzah

Dhahran

Umm Lajj

Riyadh

EGYPT

Yanbu'al Bahr

Medina

Afif

al Salam

Rabigh

Makka

Al Umayja'

Jeddah

al Ta'if

al Lith

Qal'at Bishah

al Sulayyil

RED SEA

SUDAN

al Qunfidhah

Abha

Najran

Jizan

Wuday'ah

Farasan

YEMEN ARAB REPUBLIC

ETHIOPIA

GULF OF ADEN

4

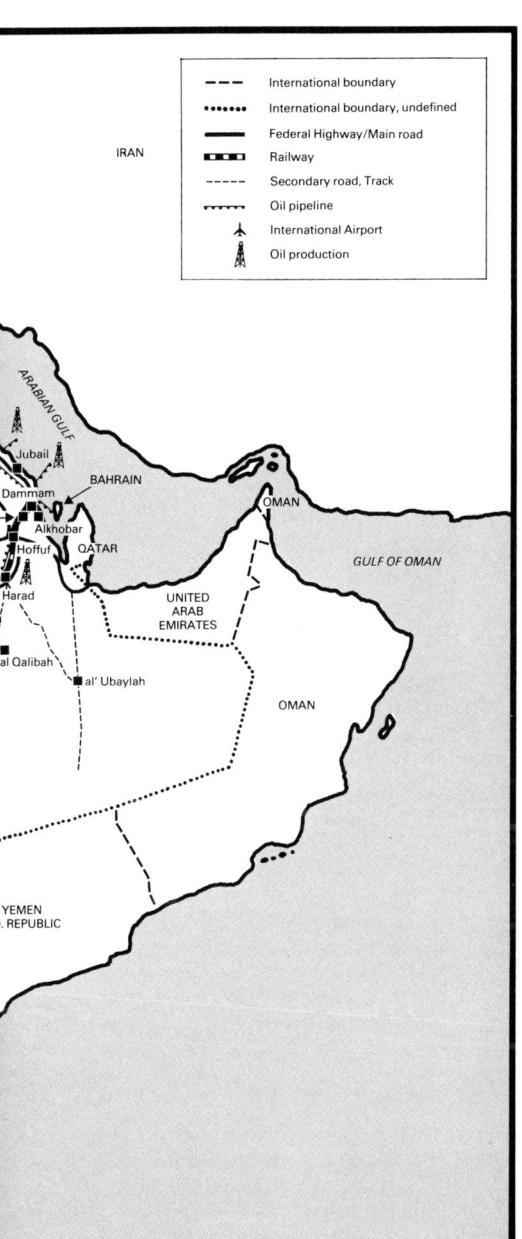

IRAN

	International boundary
	International boundary, undefined
	Federal Highway/Main road
	Railway
	Secondary road, Track
	Oil pipeline
	International Airport
	Oil production

ARABIAN GULF

Jubail

Dammam

BAHRAIN

OMAN

Alkhobar

Hoffuf QATAR

GULF OF OMAN

Harad

UNITED
ARAB
EMIRATES

al Qalibah

al' Ubaylah

OMAN

YEMEN
. REPUBLIC

Getting there

Entry regulations

Passports
Passports are required by all visitors except those Muslim pilgrims who hold special passes.

Visas
Visas are required by all visitors, except nationals of the Gulf Cooperation Council States, and must be obtained in advance. Basic requirements for obtaining a visa are:–

(a) A passport valid for a reasonable period after the issuance of a visa.

(b) A completed application form.

(c) A letter of invitation from a Saudi sponsor endorsed either by the Ministry of Foreign Affairs in Jeddah or by a Saudi Chamber of Commerce.

(d) Two photographs and the relevant fee.

British companies which are members of the Arab British Chamber of Commerce may use that organisation to obtain visas on their behalf. Those companies maintaining representation in the Kingdom and whose names appear in the British Embassy Companies' List may obtain visas direct after providing a suitable letter certified by the FCO in London as to its authenticity.

Visas will not be issued to any traveller of Israeli origin; or who has an Israeli visa stamped in his passport; or who has any other indication of a visit to Israel in his travel documents.

Vaccination regulations
A valid certificate of vaccination against yellow fever and cholera is required if arriving from an infected area. Inoculations against typhoid, tetanus, polio and hepatitis are recommended but not essential. Malarial prophylactics are

recommended for those people who will be travelling outside the main towns, especially in the South.

Health

The first health precautions that should be taken in connection with a visit to the Gulf are vaccinations. Well before your trip, make sure that your cholera shots are in order.

If there's a serious outbreak in the region (this usually happens in mid-summer) there can be a 'scare' and you may find yourself turned back or put in quarantine unless you can produce a valid certificate. Saudi Arabia around Haj time is particularly concerned about cholera. Validity is only six months and normally there is an initial shot followed a week later by a full-dose booster, so it needs some advance planning. Make sure you get the shots recorded properly on a yellow International Certificate. Actually many physicians doubt the value of cholera vaccinations (which are at most fifty per cent effective and have been known to *cause* cholera or hepatitis) and it is possible to find a doctor who'll issue an exemption certificate on such grounds as allergy, incompatibility with other prescribed drugs, or pregnancy.

Immunization against yellow fever is never asked for, unless you have arrived very recently from an infected area (Central Africa and Central America).

Other shots such as those against polio-myelitis, rabies, typhoid and tetanus are not compulsory and the actual risk of getting these diseases is too slight to justify the trouble and expense of getting them. The same goes for malaria. However, those spending time in remote open-air locations are advised to take daily doses of paludrine or less frequent doses of chloroquine. Residents for longish periods should take the advice of their personal or company physician.

To avoid being bitten by mosquitoes, which is unpleasant enough even if they are not the dreaded anopheline variety, care should be taken not to expose the flesh when they are active. This is mainly at night as the days are usually too hot. Air-conditioning and/or ceiling fans keep them at bay, otherwise muffle up completely or use Moon Tiger, an incredibly effective Japanese burning coil made from an East African plant, or Vape-mat, also Japanese, which burns a small blue tablet that keeps them at bay. Petroleum-based copies of Moon Tiger, such as Shelltox, are less successful and give some people headaches. Mosquito netting or a mosquito net are also very effective, as are insect repellents or aerosol insecticides for short-term protection. If you have been badly bitten it might be worth immediately starting a course of chloroquine. Failing all this, if you start getting an unexplained fever between one and two weeks after exposure make sure your doctor knows the details, as malaria can be serious and even fatal.

A little known and often undiagnosed disease is sand-fly fever which can be caught from sitting with feet in the sand in the cool of the day. The disease is not usually serious, but can bring on quite high fever accompanied by headache, nausea and depression. Repellent on exposed skin is advised.

Other good health advice to follow is to make sure that all the food you eat has been properly washed and/or cooked. Usually you can't be sure, as you have no control over it, but in general hotels and the better class of restaurant are very careful. If you can't help being exposed to dubious food or drink make sure you have some appropriate medicine to hand, for prophylactic use. If you have to drink dubious water, sterilizing tablets such as Halozene are advisable, but nowadays most tap water is safe (although unpleasant in taste in some places) and bottled mineral water and aerated beverages are available almost everywhere.

Jet-lag has replaced air-sickness as the main disorder associated with flying. That is, if you don't count fear of flying itself, which is far commoner than most sufferers realize. If it's any consolation, try to remember that you are not the most frightened on the plane – you are only scared, but behind those impassive looks some people are terrified. To avoid the effects of jet-lag, rest is the only cure. Let your metabolism, which is basically that of a cave-man, re-adjust to the shock of being thrust three or four hours forward in time. (That's from Europe, at least eight if you started from the USA.) For the first day do as little as possible, which is why it can make sense to arrive over a weekend or holiday, with time to rest and acclimatize before major meetings. Some experienced travellers keep their watches on the local time of their point of departure and go by that for meals and bedtime until they've had a good night's sleep. Medical science still doesn't understand jet-lag completely, but the fact that most aircraft cabins are only pressurized to an equivalent of 8,000 feet altitude means that the air you breathe is less rich in oxygen and the gases inside you expand (Boyle's Law). The effect of alcohol is greater than at sea level.

Sunburn or even mild sunstroke can be extremely painful and spoil a business trip or holiday, so stay out of the sun as much as possible, and cover up when you can't avoid it. By all means go on the beach, but for the first day out 10 or 15 minutes is ample, and build up gradually. Beware of overcast days – the ultra-violet rays can still cause sunburn so protect the back of the knees, shoulders and insteps. The face, hands, front of legs and arms can usually take more, because of previous exposure. Creams and lotions can help, but not that much. If you're out in the sun, remember to cover your head as much as possible, but without stopping the sweating process.

The body's main defence against unaccustomed heat is to sweat, so encourage this by wearing cotton, which can absorb large amounts of moisture, rather than synthetics or mixtures, which can't. If you are prone to prickly heat, as many are, dry carefully after frequent showers, use lots of baby powder (talc) and change clothes often.

Sweating lowers the skin temperature but the water and salt it consists of must be replaced, so drink a lot more than usual. A rule of thumb is to drink four pints a day when the average temperature is 20°C, and an extra pint a day for each 10° above that. The salt rule is to double your normal intake, but the body usually tells you how much it needs. When you're low, food that would normally taste too salty seems just right. Salt tablets shouldn't be necessary. If you feel faint, make a conscious effort to absorb more salt and water as dehydration is dangerous.

Currency
The currency is the Saudi Arabian Riyal (SR) which is divided into 100 Halalas.

Banknotes: SR100, SR50, SR10, SR5 and SR1.

Coins: 1 Riyal, 50 halalas, 25 halalas, 10 halalas, 5 halalas.

International Air Communications
Saudi Arabia has 22 airports of which those at Jeddah, Riyadh and Dhahran are international. Most European and Arab airlines have direct flights to the Kingdom but only Saudia, the national airline, may land at Riyadh.

Airlines
A substantial number of airlines serve the Kingdom including: Air Algerie, Air France, Air India, Alia (Royal Jordanian Airlines), Alitalia, Austrian Airlines, British Airways, Cyprus Airways, China Airways, Egypt Air, Garuda, Gulf Air, Iberian Airways, Kenya Airlines, KLM, Korean Airways, Kuwait Airways, Libyan Arab Airlines, Lufthansa, MEA, Malaysian Airlines, Nigeria Airways, Olympic Airways, Pan Am, PIA, Royal Air Maroc, SAS, Saudia, Singapore Airlines, Somali Airlines, Sudan Airways, Swissair, Syrian Arab Airlines, Thai Airways, Tunis Air, Turkish Airlines, Yemdair and Yemenia.

Land and Sea Communications
It is possible to reach Saudi Arabia by both land and sea but arrival by either means is not recommended.

Location
Saudi Arabia occupies about four fifths of the Arabian Peninsula and is bordered to the west by the Red Sea; to the north by Jordan, Iraq and Kuwait; to the east by the Arabian Gulf and Bahrain, Qatar, the UAE and Oman; and to the south by the two Yemens.

Area
The area of the Kingdom is approximately

850,000 square miles (2.2 million square kilo-
metres) which is roughly the same area as
Western Europe.

Time
GMT + 3 hours
BST + 2 hours

North America
Eastern + 8 hours
Central + 9 hours
Pacific + 11 hours

Taxis
For detailed information please refer to pages
67 – 71.

□

Climate, holidays and business hours

Climate

The weather in Saudi Arabia does come in for a lot of criticism, most of it justified, for it is one of the hottest and most humid areas of the world. Not just occasionally, but consistently, throughout a summer that must be reckoned as lasting eight months of the year (and by the standards of Northern Europe, twelve).

But in fact it's not as bad as that implies. For a start, all hotel and office rooms are air-conditioned, and the air-conditioning lowers not only the temperature, but the humidity. Cars, taxis too, usually have air-conditioners of some kind, so that very often the big problem is to adjust from the (relatively) icy hotel/office environment to the moist oven of the street at midday, or worse still to a sun-parked car with rolled-up windows, plastic seats and an untouchable steering wheel. The human body is incredibly flexible, however, and provided you follow sensible rules for acclimatization the heat and humidity shouldn't bother you.

The climate varies quite substantially from one area to another and from one season to another.

The Asir Mountains in the west of the country are the only area of the Kingdom receiving adequate rainfall as the rest of the country receives little more than 100 mm of rain annually, usually during the winter season, and is thus arid. The fierce heat in summer is aggravated along the Red Sea and Gulf Coasts by high humidity, but the interior of the country tends to be extremely dry with great fluctuations in temperature.

In Riyadh the hot months extend from May to the end of September with temperatures reaching 38 - 42C. However, the nights are relatively cool with temperatures down to the 18 - 26C. The coolest months are December, January and February with temperatures down to a maximum of 20C during the day, and a minimum of 8C at night.

In Jeddah temperatures are more uniform throughout the year with a maximum of 33 - 37C in April to November and a minimum 19 - 20C in December to March. Humidity remains high throughout the year and rainfall, which amounts to about 60 mm, tends to occur between November and February.

In the Eastern Province maximum temperatures of 42C are reached between May and October, and humidity can reach 90% during

---

Riyadh Centre) 590m (1938 ft) 24°39′N, 46°42′E
(observation period 1941 − 45)

Mean daily air temperature

	Jan	Feb	Mar	Apr	May	Jun	Jul	Aug	Sep	Oct	Nov	Dec	Year
Max (°C)	21	23	28	32	38	42	42	42	39	34	29	21	32
Min (°C)	8	9	13	18	22	25	26	24	22	16	13	9	17

Riyadh's climate is typical of its high-lying desert location, and although midday maximums are higher than along the Gulf the air quickly cools off at sunset to give diurnal ranges of some 15°C year-round. Absolute maximums and minimums recorded in the short period 45° and −7°C. In winter it frequently freezes by night with warm sunny days. A big bonus is the low humidity, especially in the hot months. Some 10 days of recordable rain each year, bringing an average of 80 mm, mainly in March and April.

Jeddah (Centre) 7m, 21°28′N, 39°10′E (observation period 1941 — 46)

Mean daily air temperature

	Jan	Feb	Mar	Apr	May	Jun	Jul	Aug	Sep	Oct	Nov	Dec	Year
Max (°C)	29	29	29	33	35	36	37	37	36	35	33	30	33
Min (°C)	19	18	19	21	23	24	26	27	25	23	22	19	23

Jeddah's position well into the Tropics and on the Red Sea means a fairly constant hot climate year round. Humidity is also steady, averaging 55% throughout the day and year, with a slight peak in September. Only five wet days and about 60 mm of rain can be expected, though it can rain enough for two years in a single day.

14

August and September. The weather between December and March is very pleasant but can be marred by occasional storms which flood the streets. Late March and early April is usually the most pleasant time of the year.

Dress

Not many business visitors dare show up for an important appointment without the obligatory suit and tie. But the suit can be ultra lightweight, and the jacket and tie can be put on shortly before the meeting and taken off immediately afterwards. A big breakthrough in recent years has been the safari suit, which is now considered smart enough for most purposes and is definitely preferable to the suit-and-tie syndrome. Meanwhile the locals stay cool in their light, well-ventilated robes, and must secretly be laughing all the way to the wardrobe at the European.

For those whose work makes it necessary the summer months must be tolerated as best they can. When it is very hot, the working day is usually quite short and starts early so the worst part of the day, usually from noon to four, can be spent relaxing in air-conditioned comfort until the temperature has dropped.

But the visitor who can do so should avoid the summer months altogether. He will find that many key personnel are away for long periods for courses or business trips and it might have made better sense to invite the people you want to see to your country. Summer trips can still be worthwhile, however, as there is less business competition and the decision-makers you meet may appreciate you more. With flights to the Gulf so frequent and cheap (in terms of other expenses) it anyway pays to go more often for short trips with specific objects rather than longer, comprehensive visits.

Ramadan and other religious festivals should also play an important part in planning a trip to Saudi Arabia. Disgruntled businessmen can sometimes be seen in hotel lobbies waiting for doors to re-open after a festival they failed to take into account. (Some didn't even know about the Thursday/Friday weekend.) So do check holiday dates before finalizing your arrangements. Be particularly careful of the combination of weekends and official holidays. If a public holiday occurs on a Sunday, Saturday will theoretically be a working day, but many top and even not-so-top people will seize the chance to take Saturday off as well, thus creating a three- or four-day holiday. A Wednesday holiday can have a similar effect by turning Thursday into a full holiday. Ramadan and the week following it are notoriously bad times for business appointments.

Public Holidays

There are no official public holidays in Saudi Arabia. However, business activity stops a few days before the end of Ramadan and recommences after the end of Eid al-Fitr; business ceases again about one week before 10th Dhu al-Hijja and restarts shortly after the end of the Eid al-Adha at the conclusion of the pilgrimage. In 1984 these holidays will occur in late June/early July and late August/early September respectively.

Business Hours

Government
0730 - 1430 – Saturday to Wednesday inclusive.

Banks
Morning Hours – Saturday to Thursday 0830 - 1200 throughout the country.
Evening Hours – Saturday to Wednesday.
1600 - 1800 – Eastern Province.
1630 - 1830 – Riyadh.
1700 - 1900 – Jeddah.

Commercial Offices

The main working hours are between 0800 and 1300 and between 1700 and 2000. However there are many variations on this theme such that work can be executed any time between 0630 and 2030. Offices close around 1300 hours on Thursday for the weekend.

The business visitor should not be put off by the presence and even participation of several other people at what he would prefer to be a private discussion. Those present may be business associates of the person in question, or simply members of his family who have called in for an informal discussion. If coffee is served it is courteous to accept it. Cups will generally be refilled automatically unless the recipient shakes his cup from side to side on returning it to the server.

Because of its refreshing informality, business can take longer than expected in Saudi Arabia. Just how much longer is a moot point, depending on the number and the nature of the people you wish to see. A useful rule of thumb would be to allow twice the amount of time you would for a similar programme in Europe or the USA.

□

History and infrastructure

History

No comprehensive study has yet been carried out on the pre-history of the Arabian Peninsula, but the earliest archaeological evidence does point to contacts between Mesopotamia and the Dilmun civilisation of Bahrain in the third millennium, which probably affected parts of Saudi Arabia's Eastern Province.

The origins of the modern state of Saudi Arabia go back to the year 1744, when Mohammad bin Abdul-Wahhab, a reformer who sought to purify and simplify Islam, came under the protection of Mohammad bin Saud, ruler of Diriyah, a small town near Riyadh. Mohammad bin Abdul-Wahhab, whose teachings are generally called Wahhabism, died in 1792, by which time the combination of his followers' religious fervour and the inspired military leadership of the Saud family, had carved out a desert kingdom centred on Diriyah. This Kingdom gained widespread power and brought under its control Damascus, Karbela, Makkah, and al Madinah before it was finally subdued by the Turks in 1838.

A Wahhabi revival soon began to spread under the leadership of a collateral branch of the Saud family. By the 1870s their power was re-established in the Nejd, though before long they received another setback when rivalry between brothers and military success by a rival Arab family, the Rashidis, caused the remaining Sauds to take refuge in Kuwait, but in 1902 the youngest Saud, Abdul-Aziz, launched a daring raid on Riyadh itself, killing the Rashidi Governor and, with only some 30 followers, seizing the city. Abdul-Aziz established himself as Emir of Riyadh while still in his early twenties, and within a few years had re-conquered his family's traditional domains in central Arabia. Fearing a further Wahhabi revival, the Ottomans launched a counter-attack, but Abdul-Aziz prevailed and even succeeded in expelling the Ottomans from Al-Hasa.

With the Ottomans crushed by World War I the only obstacle to supremacy was Sharif Hussein of Makkah, recognised by the British as King of Hejaz, leader of the Arab Revolt and companion-in-arms of T.E. Lawrence. Hussein's son Faisal became King of Iraq and the Rashidis still controlled Hail, a strategic town between Riyadh and Iraq. Abdul Aziz consolidated his power by taking Hail and soon turned his thoughts to the Hejaz, where in 1924 Hussein virtually claimed the title of Caliph after the new Turkish Republic formally abolished the Caliphate. This aroused the wrath of the powerful Wahhabi faction and Abdul Aziz invaded the Hejaz, and in 1926 declared himself King of the Hejaz. In 1927 Abdul Aziz was recognised by Britain as independent ruler of most of Arabia, pledging to respect Britain's treaty relationships with the 10 Gulf Sheikhdoms and Oman, and international recognition soon followed. Five years later he proclaimed the Kingdom of Saudi Arabia, united the Nejd, Hejaz and Al-Hasa, and thus virtually completed establishment of a unified modern state.

The Kingdom's first oil concession was awarded in 1933 and oil was discovered in 1938. Development was delayed by World War II, but oil revenues began to grow rapidly in the post-war years with the establishment of Aramco as operator.

King Abdul Aziz, known inaccurately in the West as Ibn Saud, died in 1953 and was succeeded by his eldest son, Saud. In 1964 pressure from the royal princes, the newly formed Council of Ministers, and the religious leaders forced him to abdicate in favour of his brother, Faisal.

Under King Faisal's leadership, Saudi Arabia soon regained its economic stability and its international prestige grew rapidly. Oil revenues increased at an astonishing pace as production and price levels rose in the latter half of the sixties and the first half of the seventies. King Faisal confounded his critics by showing that strict adherence to the traditional Islam was compatible with material progress, including modern education. Personally austere, he was respected throughout the Arab world, and beyond.

His assassination by a mentally unbalanced nephew was a severe blow for Saudi Arabia, the Arab cause and world stability, but fortunately his brother Khaled kept up the tradition of wise leadership. King Khaled died in June 1982 and was succeeded by his brother Fahd who had provided substantial support as Crown Prince. Today, following reductions in both oil prices and production levels, the Kingdom is undergoing a period of consolidation under King Fahd's leadership.

Head of State, Constitution, Government

Official Title of Country
The Kingdom of Saudi Arabia

Head of State
His Majesty King Fahd bin AbdulAziz al Saud, who is also Prime Minister and President of the Council of Ministers.

Government

Head of State/Prime Minister
King Fahd bin AbdulAziz.

First Deputy Premier & Commander of the National Guard
Prince Abdullah bin AbdulAziz.

Second Deputy Premier & Minister of Defence and Aviation
Prince Sultan bin AbdulAziz.

Agriculture and Water
*AbdulRahman bin AbdulAziz
bin Hassan al Shaikh.*

Commerce
Sulaiman AbdulAziz al Solaim.

Communications
Hussain Ibrahim alMansouri.

Education
AbdulAziz alAbdullah al Khuwaiter.

Finance and Economy
Mohammed Ali AbalKhail.

Foreign Affairs
Prince Saud alFaisal.

Health (as at 19/3/83 - Acting
Dr. Ghazi alGosaibi)

Higher Education
Hassan bin Abdullah alShaikh.

Industry and Electricity
Dr. Ghazi AbdulRahman alGosaibi.

Information
Ali Hassan alShaer

Interior
Prince Naif bin AbdulAziz.

Justice
Ibrahim bin Mohammad bin Ibrahim alShaikh.

Labour and Social Affairs
Ibrahim bin Abdullah alAngari.

Municipal & Rural Affairs (Acting at 19/3/83)
Prince Miteb bin AbdulAziz.

Petroleum and Minerals
Ahmad Zaki Yamani.

Pilgrimage Affairs & Awqaf
Abdul Wahhab Ahmad Abdul Wasie.

Planning
Hisham Nazer.

Posts, Telegraphs and Telecommunications
Alawi Darwish Kayyal.

Public Works & Housing
Prince Miteb bin AbdulAziz.

Constitution
There is no written constitution as ultimate authority is considered to lie in the hands of God. The duty of the Monarch is to ensure the observation of God's Law, the Sharia. In this he is advised by a Council of Ministers which was formed in 1958.

The Council of Ministers' powers are extensive and include "the determination of internal, foreign, financial, economic, education and defence policies in addition to all public affairs of the Kingdom." However, no decision of the Council of Ministers comes into effect until sanctioned by the king.

Under the Council of Ministers are four departments, namely; the Secretariat General; the Controller of State Accounts; the Board of Grievance; and the Department of Experts.

Population

The population of Saudi Arabia is now estimated to be in excess of 10 million, with the number of Saudi nationals being between 7 and 8 million. Estimates indicate the presence of some 2.5 million foreign workers of many nationalities, as compared with about 1.75 million economically active Saudis. The current Five-Year Development Plan concentrates to a substantial extent or increasing the number of skilled Saudi nationals in order to reduce dependence on foreign labour.

Since the early 1970s there has been a substantial population movement towards the major cities but current government policies are aimed at encouraging individuals to return to the outlying areas of the Kingdom.

Recent estimates suggest the population of Riyadh, the capital, to be about 1.2 million; Jeddah 1.15 million; and the three Eastern towns of Dammam, Al Khobar and Dhahran 0.45 million.

National Flag

Green, with the text of the Shahada (There is no god but God and Mohammad is His Prophet) in white above a white sword.

Religion

Islam – Saudi Arabia is the homeland of the Islamic Faith and the practice of all other religions is forbidden.

Islam is more than a religion, it is a civil and penal code. In most respects the visitor to Saudi Arabia will not find his pattern of behaviour altered too drastically. Obvious exceptions apply to the prohibition of alcohol, and food during the month of fasting. However, as a matter of common courtesy and common sense, visitors are recommended to respect customs and traditions which form an integral part of Muslim society.

Language

The language of the Kingdom is Arabic. All official documents between business entities, both Saudi and foreign, and Ministries and Government Agencies must be in Arabic. However, many government officials and Saudi businessmen have been educated abroad, and English as a medium for conversation is almost universally acceptable.

Customs

Unless addressing members of the Royal Family normal western forms of address are accepted and used. Care should be taken in the offering of gifts to government officials as the intention may occasionally be misinterpreted or taken for more than a straightforward expression of goodwill. Handshakes are a customary greeting and the right hand should always be used for consuming food of any kind.

Lady visitors and wives accompanying visiting (as opposed to resident) businessmen will find problems in obtaining visas, restrictions in their movements within the country and should not be surprised to find that they are not included in the invitations to official and business receptions. Unaccompanied lady visitors for purposes of business or tourism will find it extremely difficult to obtain entry visas for Saudi Arabia. Female employment in the Kingdom is restricted to certain professions – nurses, doctors, and teachers for example.

Gulf Arabic – common words and phrases

The Arabic equivalents given here are in spoken standard Arabic, the most useful forms for the average expatriate who wishes to learn something of the language. Where a local alternative is in common use in the Gulf this is given in parentheses.

Hello	As-salam'alaikum (reply: wa'alaikum as-salam) Marhaba (reply: marhaba)

Welcome	Ahlan wa sahlan (*or simply* Ahlan)
Good morning	Sabah al-khair (reply: sabah an-nur)
Good evening	Masa al-khair (reply: masa an-nur)
Good night	Tisbah alakhair
Good-bye	Ma'a Salama
How are you?	Kair al-hal? (Ishlonak *or* Shlonak?)
Well, thank you	Bikhair al-hamdu lillah
Thank you	Shukran (Ahsant)
Don't mention it	Afwan
Please	Min fadlak *(to a man)* Min fadlik *(to a woman)*
Yes	Na'am
No	La
If God wills	In sha allah
This	Hadha
That	Dhalik

Pronouns

I	Ana
You (m)	Ant
You (f)	Anti
He	Hiwa
She	Hiya
We	Nahan
You (pl)	Antum
They	Hum

Prepositions

With	Ma'a
In	Fi
To, for belongs to	Li
Above/up	Fawq
Under/down	Taht
Between	Bayn
Towards	Ila
Before	Qabl
After	Ba'd
Behind	Wara
In front of	Amam
From	Min
Near	Qarib min
Far (from)	Ba'id (an)

Numerals

One	Wahed

Two	٢	Ithnain
Three	٣	Thalatha
Four	٤	Arba'a
Five	٥	Khamsa
Six	٦	Sitta
Seven	٧	Sab'a
Eight	٨	Thamania
Nine	٩	Tis'a
Ten	١٠	'Ashra
Eleven	١١	Ahad'ashar
Twelve	١٢	Ithna'ashar
Thirteen	١٣	Thalathat'ashar
Fourteen	١٤	'Arba'at'ashar
Fifteen	١٥	Khamasat'ashar
Sixteen	١٦	Sittat'ashar
Seventeen	١٧	Saba'at'ashar
Eighteen	١٨	Thamaniat'ashar
Nineteen	١٩	Tis'at'ashar
Twenty	٢٠	'Ishreen
Twentyone		Wahed wa'ishreen (etc)
Thirty		Thalatheen
Forty		Arba'een
Fifty		Khamseen
Sixty		Sitteen
Seventy		Sab'een
Eighty		Thamaneen
Ninety		Tis'een
One hundred		Mi'a
Two hundred		Mi'atain
Five hundred		Khams mi'a
One thousand		Alf
One million		Mily'un

Ordinals

1st	Al-awwal
2nd	Ath-thani
3rd	Ath-thalith
4th	Ar-rabi
5th	Al-Khamis
6th	As-sadis
7th	As-sabi'
8th	Ath-thamin
9th	At-tasi'
10th	Al-ashir
11th	Al-hadi'ashar
12th etc.	Ath-thani'ashar

Time

Day	Yawm
Week	Usbu'
Month	Shahr
Year	Sana
Morning	Sabah
Afternoon	Ba'ad adh-dhuhr
Evening	Masa
Night	Layl
Tomorrow	Ghadan (Bukra)
Yesterday	Ams
Today	Al-yawm
This morning	Sabah al-yawm
This afternoon	Ba'ad dhuhr al-yawm
Tonight	Masa al-yawm
Tomorrow morning	Bukra fi sabah
What time is it?	Kam as-saa?
It is –	As-sa'a + number
Half past –	Wa nusf
Now	Alan (Al-hin)
Immediately	Halan

Days of the week

Sunday	Yawm al-ahad
Monday	Yawm al-ithnayn
Tuesday	Yawm ath-thulatha
Wednesday	Yawm al-arbi'a
Thursday	Yawm al-khamees
Friday	Yawm al-jum'a
Saturday	Yawm as-sabt

Months

January	Yana'ir
February	Fibra'ir
March	Mars
April	Abril
May	Mayo
June	Yuniyo
July	Yuliyo
August	Augustus
September	Sebtember
October	Oktober
November	Nofember
December	Desember

Colours

Black	Aswad
White	Abyad
Red	Ahmar

Green	Akhdar
Blue	Azraq
Yellow	Asfar
Brown	Bunni

Travel

Car	Sayyara
Taxi	Taksi
Bus	Autobees
Ship	Bakhira
Boat	Lanch, Safina
Plane	Tayara
Take me to . . .	Khudni ila
Stop	Qif
Here	Huna (Hini)
There	Hunalik (Hinak)
Left	Yasaar
Right	Yameen
Straight on	Dughri
North	Shamal
East	Sharq
South	Junub
West	Gharb
Centre	Markez
The road to	At-tariq ila –

Interrogatives

When?	Mata?
Who?	Man?
What?	Madha? (Shu, ash)
Which?	Ai?
Why?	Limadha?
Where? Where is?	Ain? (Wain? Fain?)
How?	Kaif? (Shlon?)
How much?	Bikam?
How many?	Kam?

Nationalities

British	Ingleezi (a)
American	Amreeki (a)
French	Firansi (a)
German	Almani (a)
Dutch	Hollandi (a)
Italian	Itali (a)
Austrian	Namsawi (a)
Danish	Danmarki (a)
Swedish	Sawaydi (a)
Norwegian	Nurweji (a)
Belgian	Balijiki (a)

Swiss	Swisseri (a)
Spanish	Isbani (a)

Places

Pharmacy	Saydiliya/farmaciya
Doctor	Tabeeb
Hospital	Mustashfa
Police	Ash-shurta
Grocery	Baqala
Hotel	Funduq/ootel
Embassy	Sifara
Ministry	Wizara
Company	Sharika
Airport	Matar
Port	Mina
Island	Jazira
Sea	Bahr
Office	Maktab
House	Bayt
Home	Manzil
Square	Maydan
Street	Shari'
Palace	Qasr
Mosque	Jami
Building	Binaya
Oilfield	Haql naft
Restaurant	Mat'am
Toilet	Hammam

Food

Food	Akl
Bread	Khubz
Butter	Zubda
Meat	Lahm
Fish	Samak
Chicken	Dajaj
Mutton	Kharoof
Rice	Aruzz
Salad	Salata
Water	Ma'i
Mineral water	Ma'i madani
Glass	Kas
Juice	Asir
Tea	Shai
Coffee	Qahwa
Sugar	Sukkar
Salt	Milh
Pepper	Filfil

Adjectives

Good	Tayyib (Zein)
Bad	Ma tayyib (Ma-zein)
Very good	Tayyib kathir
Beautiful	Jamil
Fine, OK	Tamam
Many	Kathir
Few	Qalil
Hot	Harr
Cold	Barid

Conversations

What is your name?	Ma esmak? (Smesmak?)
My name is –	Ismi –
Please help yourself	Tafaddal *(to a man)*
Come in, sit down etc.	Tafaddali *(to a woman)*
I want/would like	Ana urid
Is Mr – in?	As-sayyid – mawjud?
When will he come?	Mata yaji?
I'll wait	Ana andhurhu
Is there any?	–mawjud? (–fi?) or (–shi?)
No, there isn't	La, ghair mawjud (la, ma fi)
I'll come back	Ana raji'
How much does this cost?	Bikam hadha (m)? Bikam hadhi (f)?
That's too expensive	Hatha kath/r
I'll give you . . .	U'teek . . .
The bill please	Al-hisab min fadlak (m) Al-hisab min fadlik (f)
I don't speak Arabic	Ana la atakallam arabi
I don't read Arabic	Ana la a'rah arabi
I know only a little Arabic	Ana a'rif shwaiyet arabi bas
Do you speak English?	Tatakallam ingleezi?
Please speak slowly	Takallam/i ala mahlak/ik, min fadlak/ik
I don't understand	Ma fahimt
Forbidden	Mamnu'
Can I speak to the boss	Mumkin atakallam ma'a al-mudir?

Is there a telephone near here?	Yujad tilifun qareeb min hun?
May I use your telephone?	Mumkin asta'mil tilifunkum?
How do you say this in Arabic?	Ma hadha fil arabi? (Aysh fil arabi?)
Where are you from?	Min ain ant (i)?
I know Cairo well	Ana a'rif al-qahira kathir
I like Bahrain	A'jabatni bahrain
Are you a Muslim?	Ant(i) muslim (a)?
Have you been to Mecca?	Ant hajji?
I'm a Christian	Ana maseehi (a)
Do you have children?	'Andak awlad?
I have six sons	'Andi sittet sibyan
That's wonderful	Ma sha allah
I have only one wife	'Andi zawja waheda bas
Please tell my Embassy where I am	Min fadlak qul li sifarati ain ana
I'm innocent	Ma 'amilt shai
Go away	Halla anni
No, thanks	Shukran
Excuse me, I'm busy	'Adharni, ana mashgul

Gulf English – common words and phrases

A number of words of Arabic origin (and to a lesser extent derived from Persian and other languages) have passed into common or technical usage among English-speaking expatriates living in the Gulf countries. For the most part they describe man-made objects or ideas as well as natural phenomena peculiar to the region and have no exact English equivalent. In some cases there is a jocular undertone to their use. The following list is by no means exhaustive. In many cases, alternative spellings are to be found.

Abbaya Thin black covering worn over a woman's dress.

Abra Ferry used to cross the Khor (qv) between Dubai and Deira.

AC Air conditioning.

Allah The sole Deity of Islam.

Amir, Emir Title used by Gulf rulers, particularly in Bahrain and Qatar. Original sense, army commander.

Aqal, Iqal Rope-like headband, usually black, that holds the *Kufiya* in place. Also the cord used to hobble the feet of a camel.

Ashura The tenth day of the month of Muharram (qv), a day of deepest mourning for Shi'a Muslims. (October 17, 1983)

Ayatollah A senior Shi'a divine, recognized as an authority on legal and moral questions.

Badquir, badgir Wind-towers, used to cool houses. This ingenious architectural device originates from Iran and was brought to Dubai by Persian merchants.

Baladiya Municipal authority, responsible in most Gulf states for town planning, etc.

Barasti Reeds fastened together to make a fence or simple house.

Batula Beak-like mask worn in public by Gulf women.

Bedu Nomadic tribesman of Arabia, Bedouin. In Arabic *bedu* is the plural form of 'Bedouin', but in Gulf expat. usage it is used as a singular noun, or adjectively as 'bedu traditions', and has replaced the word Bedouin.

Bisht A man's light cloak, worn over a dish-dasha or thaub.

Boom, Bum A large dhow with sharp stern.

Bukra Tomorrow, in jocular usage as Spanish manana, often used with Inshallah (qv).

Dhow Any traditional wooden Gulf craft. The etymology of the word dhow is disputed, and certainly no current vessel is known as a dhow in Arabic, the general equivalent being 'lanch' (from English launch).

Dishdasha Long comfortable cotton robe worn by Arab men in the Gulf states. The colour and small variations in tailoring style can tell an expert much about the wearer's social and geographic background.

Diwan Reception room of a palace or large private house. Also used to mean a group of advisers of a ruler, or his personal secretariat. Connected etymologically to the word 'divan' and the French 'douane'.

Donum A measure of land area, varying in size between 900 and 2,500 sq m.

Eid Any Muslim festival holiday, particularly the Eid al-Fitr which marks the end of Ramadan (qv). (July 12, 1983)

Expat Common abbreviation for 'expatriate', a foreign worker or resident, usually in the sense of European or North American.

Falaj A man-made underground water channel.

Farrash A male domestic servant, particularly one concerned with laying out and sweeping carpets.

Feddah Measure of land area about 4,200 sq m.

Garden Agricultural smallholding, whose owners often live in nearby towns and use it for family picnics at week-ends. 'Gardens' are a particular feature of life in Bahrain and Qatar.

Ghishura A black veil worn by women.

Ghuta A man's cloth headcloth.

Haj, Haji The pilgrimage to Makkah made during the month of Dhul-Hujjah and culminating in the Feast of the Sacrifice on the tenth of that month. Making the Haj pilgrimage is one of the five 'pillars' of Islam, and incumbent on every Muslim who can afford it. A person who has made the pilgrimage is entitled to be called Haj, Haji in the vocative case.

Halwa Sweetmeat, usually made of sesame oil, sugar and flavourings.

Hamour One of the most popular fishes caught in the Gulf, rock cod or grouper.

Haram   An act forbidden by Islam such as drinking wine or eating pork.

Hijra   The start of the Islamic calendar era (see The Islamic Calendar page 8).

Hotel   In the *suq* (qv) area the word hotel is often used to connote a cheap restaurant, an Indian linguistic influence.

Imam   To a Sunni (qv), an imam (small i) is a leader of communal prayer in a mosque. To a Shi'ite (qv), an Imam (capital I) is one of the 12 spiritual leaders of his sect.

Islam   The religion of the Muslims, literally meaning 'submission (to God)'.

Jebel   A hill, or slight eminence.

Jebeli   A highlander, particularly one from the Dhofar province of Oman.

Jihad   A holy war by Muslims against infidels.

Kafiya, Kufiya   A man's cloth headdress.

Khalij   A gulf, more particularly the Gulf, commonly used in business names.

Khor   A creek, probably derived from a Persian root meaning 'eat'. Several settlements in the GCC countries, notably Dubai and Sharjah, owe their existence to such creeks, which were natural harbours, and still are for traditional vessels. Early travellers, and even some modern ones have mistaken these curious phenomena for rivers.

Khanjar, Khunyar   An Omani or Yemeni dagger, usually in an ornate silver scabbard.

Koran, Quran   The Holy Book of Islam. To a Muslim, the Koran is the Word of God.

Majlis   The reception room in an Arab home. Also a public reception given by a notable.

Minaret   A slender turret adjacent to a mosque from which the muezzin (qv) makes the call to prayer.

Mosque   A place of communal worship for Muslims.

Mubarek   A greeting used on a festival

occasion, usually 'Eid Mubarak' (Congratulations on the Holiday).

Muezzin   The person who makes the call to prayer from a minaret (qv) at prescribed times of the day and night. In Sunni (qv) mosques this is done by a non-musical if stylized proclamation; Shi'a muezzins chant the call.

Muharram   The first month of the Islamic Year, a month of religious mourning for Shi'a Muslims (qv). (Starts October 8, 1983)

Muslim   A follower of Islam (The older term 'Muhammadan' should be avoided).

Qadi, Cadi, Kadi   A relgious judge who administers the Shari'a (qv).

Qibla, Kibla   The direction from the point of prayer to Makkah. Mosques are always built in alignment to the qibla.

Ramadan   The ninth month of the Islamic calendar, a month of fasting and self-purification.

Rupee   The Indian Rupee, then from 1959 a special convertible Gulf Rupee, were the main units of currencey in Kuwait until 1961 and in Qatar and the UAE until 1966, after which national currencies were issued, but the term rupee lingers on among the older inhabitants to denote the new currency regardless of differences in actual value. This is particularly true of Dubai, where traders seem to prefer the term rupee (pronounced 'rupiah') to the correct name dirham.

Sabkha   Salt flats, a common feature along the Gulf coast.

Sambuk   A traditional pearling boat.

Shaikh, Sheikh, Shaykh   A title of respect, originally given to a tribal chief, without precise meaning. In modern Gulf usage it is usually applied to any male member of the ruling family. Feminine 'shaika'.

Shamal, Shimal   A strong northerly north-westerly wind, usually hot.

Sharia   The revealed or canonical law of Islam.

Shahada The Muslim profession of faith. 'There is no god but Allah, and Muhammad is the Messenger of Allah'.

Shi'a A major branch of Islam whose adherents believe in a system of hereditary Imams, the first of whom was Ali, the son-in-law of the Prophet Muhammad. In the Gulf countries most Shi'a Muslims (Shi'ites) are 'Twelvers' who believe that there have been 12 Imams, the last of whom is the Imam of the Age, whose revelation will mark the Day of Judgement. There are many Shi'ites in Bahrain and most Iranians in the Gulf are Shi'ites.

Sunni The main branch of Islam, whose adherents practice what is generally a simpler and more fundamental form of the religion. Except for Bahrain and Iraq most native-born Arabs in the Gulf are Sunni.

Suq, Suk A traditional Arab bazaar or shopping area.

Thaub A man's long white dress, usually buttoned up at the neck, as opposed to a dishdasha, which is usually open at the neck and may be of other colours.

Wadi A river in desert country, for most of the year a dry river bed. Also used of valleys.

Wahhabi A puritanical form of Islam that originated in Saudi Arabia in the nineteenth century, preaching strict obedience of the Koran. The Wahhabis themselves use the term, *Muwahhidun* (Unitarians).

Wali Provincial governor, particularly in Oman.

Wasmi Seasonal rain.

Principal Towns/Ports/Airports

Principal Towns
Riyadh (population 1.2 million) is the chief town of the Central Province and is the seat of Government. All Ministries, except Foreign Affairs, and most public agencies are there. Riyadh was the city attacked by Abdul Aziz alSaud in 1902 and from which he ventured in the course of unifying the substantial area now known as Saudi Arabia.

Jeddah (population 1.15 million), the country's diplomatic and commercial centre and chief port, is the administrative capital of the North-Western (Hejaz) Province and the largest city on the Red Sea. An ancient settlement, it is the gateway for pilgrims arriving either by sea or air. Other important cities in the Hejaz are Makkah (population 0.4 million), known as 'the Blessed', and Madinah (population 0.23 million) 'the Radiant', the two holiest cities of Islam, whose population increases enormously every year during the pilgrimage season. Ta'if (population 0.25 million),on the highway to Riyadh, also becomes very crowded in the summer months as people escape to the mountains from the heat and humidity of the Red Sea Plain. Halfway between Jeddah and the head of the Red Sea is Yanbu, where a new industrial city is being established including oil, gas and petrochemical complexes.

The chief towns of the Eastern Province (Al-Hasa) are Dammam, Al Khobar and Dhahran (population 0.45 million in total), which can today be considered almost a conurbation. Dammam is the country's second largest port, Al Khobar a modern commercial centre. Both exist primarily to serve the oil industry, which is almost exclusively in the Eastern Province, with its centre at Dhahran. In addition a substantial new industrial city is being built in Jubail where a large number of major projects are being developed.

Other important towns in the Kingdom include Abha, Khamis Mushayt and Jizan (all in the south west of the Kingdom); Buraidah and Onaiza (in the North Central Area of Qassim); and Tabuk (in the North West). In addition a number of new military cities have been established in important locations around the country.

Ports

The two major sea ports of the Kingdom are Jeddah and Dammam through which 36 million tons and 25 million tons respectively passed during 1982. Other important ports include Jizan, Yanbu and Jubail whose combined throughput is substantially less at approximately 10 million tons.

Airports

There are 22 airports in the Kingdom but only those in Jeddah, Riyadh and Dhahran are international.

King Abdul Aziz International Airport in Jeddah has two terminals – the south for all Saudia flights and the north for all international airline flights. The two terminals are about 20 Kms and 35 Kms respectively from the city centre.

Riyadh's present airport is situated to the north east of the city about 3 Kms from the city centre and only serves Saudia flights. No international airlines land there. During 1984 the new King Khaled International Airport will come into use and this is situated about 40 Kms North West of the city centre. It is anticipated that international airlines will be permitted to use this airport.

Dhahran Airport serves a large number of airlines and is situated some 8 Kms south of Dhahran and about 25 Kms from Dammam and 17 Kms from Al Khobar. There are separate terminals for domestic and international flights which are about 1 Km apart.

Minimum check-in time at all three airports is 60 mins, but at peak times two hours is recommended for international flights.

□

The economy

The economy of Saudi Arabia has undergone substantial change during the past two years as a direct result of the reduction in oil production and prices. These reductions have naturally had a detrimental effect on the domestic economy.

The challenge which Saudi Arabia now has to face, therefore, is whether it can readjust to a period of fiscal restraint. After a long period of spending on a grand scale such a readjustment must be difficult but all the signs indicate a satisfactory transition is taking place.

The budget announced early in 1983 amounted to SR260 billion, an amount approximately SR16 billion in excess of actual expenditure the previous year, and SR35 billion in excess of anticipated revenue. Many observers outside Saudi Arabia anticipated a drop in the budget amount but with admirable logic the Saudis argued this might have had a detrimental effect on society and this they wish to avoid.

Given the reduction in income it was inevitable that many development projects would be affected. However, a number of ministerial pronouncements during the past twelve months have indicated an intention to follow the current five year plan (1980-85) through to fruition – albeit some projects will take longer to be completed.

During the past ten years the country has undergone a profound physical transformation. The government has been responsible to a substantial extent for this by providing all the basic infrastructure and by encouraging and supporting national industrial and agricultural development. In short, the surpluses from oil have, to a large extent, been ploughed back into the country.

Now, after many years of both direct and indirect involvement by the government, it wants to see increased participation from the private sector – and this is where it believes the future of the Kingdom lies. There will continue to be government support for private business, as long as it remains relevant, and the two sides will maintain a close association, but the full development of the private sector is the ultimate aim.

Oil and Gas

With reserves of oil officially estimated in late 1979 at 167bn barrels (enough to sustain production for another 50 years at the rate of 8.5m b/d), Saudi Arabia accounts for some 25% of world reserves. In 1976 the country displaced the United States as the second largest oil producer, topped only by the USSR, and for some years it has been by far the largest exporter. The Kingdom's preponderant weight in the oil market stems from the fact that its discovered reserves expand faster than they are depleted.

The original concession to explore for oil in Saudi Arabia was granted to Standard Oil of California, later joined by Texaco, Exxon and Mobil, the first three with 30% interests, the last with 10%. The four jointly formed Aramco, the Arabian American Oil Company, with headquarters in Dhahran.

Aramco is now completely Saudi owned. The takeover started in 1974, when the Kingdom acquired 25% participation, which soon expanded to 60%. Now, $1.5bn has reportedly been paid to Aramco's four American partners for the remaining 40% interest.

Over 90% of Saudi oil production is exported as crude, but refining capacity is being greatly expanded, both to meet growing domestic demand and to increase the value added of exported oil. Over the next decade, Saudi Arabia plans to build by far the largest and most sophisticated refining capacity in the Middle East. Five joint-venture export-oriented refineries with an initial capacity of some 900,000 b/d have been agreed upon. Petromin (Saudi Arabia's General Petroleum and Mineral Organization) and Mobil will build a $2bn, 250,000 b/d refinery at Yanbu, on the Red Sea. It will be fed with crude from the giant Ghawar

field near the Gulf by a projected 1.85m b/d
east-west pipeline. Another 250,000 b/d refinery,
to be built in collaboration with Royal Dutch
Shell, is planned for Jubail, on the Gulf. Like the
Yanbu plant, it will concentrate on the lighter
products – naptha, kerosene and gasolene –
which will comprise 60% of its output.

Natural gas (current reserves 116 trillion cu
ft or more than 4% of the world's total) was
discovered in Saudi Arabia before oil but it is
only in recent years that its exploitation has
commenced. During the past five years, expen-
ditures to lay the base for a massive gas-
gathering scheme whose eventual cost will
exceed $18bn have been second only to those
invested in the development of crude oil
resources.

To help meet the needs of growing domestic
consumption, currently increasing at an annual
rate of 25%, a 170,000 b/d refinery is being
built at Yanbu in collaboration with a Japanese
firm, Chiyoda Petrostar.

Downstream from oil, some $14bn worth of
primary petrochemical plants will be built over
the next six years. The largest of these, a joint-
venture with Shell, will be a $3bn plant in Jubail
producing some 656,000 tons of ethylene as of
1986.

Industry and mining

Since 1974, Saudi Arabia has embarked on an
ambitious industrialization programme as a
means of lessening long-term dependence on
hydrocarbons, and today this sector occupies a
still small but fast-growing segment of the
Kingdom's economy. Industries which require
high capital investment or have strategic value
are kept in Government hands. Thus, it is a state
agency, SABIC (Saudi Arabian Basic Industries
Corporation), which joined with Korf Stahl AG
of West Germany to build and operate a direct
reduction steel plant (annual capacity 850,000
tons) at Jubail, as well as an associated rolling
mill. Both started production in 1983.

The same partnership has undertaken the
modernization and expansion of Jeddah's
existing rolling mill, whose productive capacity
for steel bars in 1983 was 150,000 tons. The

output of the two plants will make the country self-sufficient in basic steel reinforcing bars.

Food is also a sensitive area and it is the state which is the sole owner of the Grain Silos and Flour Mills Organization, established in 1972. The Organization already operates four grain silo complexes and three wheat flour and animal feed complexes. During the Third Development Plan, it will build two additional grain storage, flour and animal feed mill complexes.

In other fields, the Government is attempting to foster both private and foreign investment, the latter on condition that Saudi partners are included in the venture. Generous inducements are offered to encourage the establishment of industries that are relevent to Saudi market demand, and an increasing number of Saudi businessmen are turning from trading to industry. One of the largest private projects is the National Pipe Company, near Dhahran, run in collaboration with Japanese interests. Other either wholly Saudi-owned or joint-ventures include plants to produce chemicals, aluminium, plastics, air conditioners, electric power, cement and fertiliser, as well as truck assembly plant.

Wider ownership of local industries is presently being encouraged and it seems probable that during 1984 a number of privately owned companies will be public. As there were 1,384 productive factories in the Kingdom in mid-1983 there would appear to be substantial potential for this policy.

As regards minerals, substantial exploration has been carried out and some 700 mineral deposits have been found in the Kingdom. Among those minerals found are gold, silver, copper, lead, zinc, iron, phosphates, beryl, fluorite, magnesium, salt and sulphur and certain radio-active minerals.

The government announced early in 1983 a policy of exploitation of some of these minerals including iron ore from the Wadi Sawawin in the north west; gold, and its associated minerals, from Mahd adh Dhabab north of al Madinah; copper from the Zaid region about 350 Kms north east of Jeddah; and bauxite from between Hail and Qassim in the north central area.

Not only are minerals to be found on-shore but also in the Red Sea where the Saudi-Sudan Red Sea Exploitation Commission has found silver, zinc and copper in substantial quantities.

Given the reduction in oil production and price, the Kingdom's other mineral resources should provide a substantial alternative source of income to enable the government to satisfactorily fulfil its development obligations.

Agriculture, Water and Fishing

With nearly 90% of foodstuffs consumed in the country imported, a determined drive has been launched to bolster local food production. In the Third Development Plan no less than SR 7.9bn has been allocated to the agricultural sector.

At present 0.24% of the Kingdom's land area is under cultivation, representing only one-third of the 2 million hectares that could be extensively farmed. Irrigation is the main problem and, under the new plan, half the funds for the development of water resources are to be directed to agriculture.

Despite the diminution of small farming and the drop in crop yields, large-scale agricultural enterprises have been doing very well. Since 1978, about 20 commercial dairy farms have been established and more are planned, including what will be the Middle East's largest integrated dairy farm. Egg and chicken production has doubled, and it is hoped that 50% of demand will be met locally by 1985.

New attention is also being paid to developing the fisheries industry. Despite a 1,320 km coastline, Saudi Arabia has made less effort to develop its potential than have its neighbours with their trading and pearling traditions. The FAO has estimated that the annual catch could be as high as 500,000 tons, whereas it is now 16,000. In 1980 the Saudi Fisheries Company was established by the Government to expand the catch and develop fish processing and marketing.

Banking and Finance

In recent years there have been substantial developments in the banking sector such that there are now in excess of 420 bank branches around the Kingdom. At the time of writing, these branches belong to a total of ten commercial banks in the Kingdom, including the United Saudi Commercial Bank which opened its doors in 1983, with total assets in excess of SR110 billion (US$ 32 billion).

However, as the economy slows down so inevitably does the growth of the banking sector. According to statistics issued by the Saudi Arabian Monetary Agency (SAMA) the rate of growth in the first six months of 1982 was only 14%, compared with 23% for the whole of 1981. The decline in lending was more dramatic with a decrease from a 37.7% growth rate in 1980/81 to 15% in 1981/82.

SAMA continues to maintain strict control over the banking sector and over the Saudi Riyal. The restrictions imposed on the banks will tend to have an adverse effect on their profitability in the immediate future, but reduced activity will inevitably provide them with time to consolidate. Although there are no exchange controls in effect in the Kingdom, SAMA has a marked preference for keeping riyals in the country. Regulations issued in early 1983 discouraging banks from syndicating riyal denominated loans offshore (usually in Bahrain) are very much part of this policy.

Increasing control by SAMA during the next year seems most likely given the change in economic circumstances during 1983. In the long run such control can only be beneficial, although the bankers themselves may not see it that way.

Main Exports/Imports and Main Trading Partners

The major export of the Kingdom is oil. Other exports include hides, plastic products and jewellery. In addition a substantial re-export market exists in equipment and foodstuffs.

The major imports into the Kingdom are cement, grains (especially barley), motor vehicles and equipment, livestock (especially sheep) and a wide range of dry and frozen foods.

The Kingdom's major trading partners are Japan, USA, South Korea, France, Holland, Great Britain, Italy, West Germany, Spain and Belgium.

Customs regulations

Standard rate of duty ad valorem
3% on most goods.
No duty on transit goods.

Exemptions

Government departments
No

Oil companies
No

Food
No

Books, periodicals, newspapers
N/A

Gold and silver bullion
N/A

Livestock
N/A

Others
N/A

Licence required for
Arms, ammunition, medicines, plants, fruits,
seeds and livestock

Prohibited items
Liquor, pork products, meat not slaughtered in
accordance with Muslim law

Higher duty items
N/A

Exemption for commercial samples up to
reasonable value (about $200)
No (unless 'unsaleable')

Refund of duty paid on high value samples when
re-exported (provision for Bank guarantee)
Yes (coloured photographs of high-value
samples required)

Duty on re-exports
No

Other regulations
No

Telecommunications Facilities

Saudi Arabia now has one of the most sophisticated telecommunications networks in the world. International dialling facilities are available to most subscribers, and Telex services are excellent. There are public telephone and telex facilities in most towns. Cable facilities also remain available.

All telephone numbers in the Kingdom are now of seven digits. Dialling from one city in the Kingdom to another is achieved by dialling 0, followed by the city code and the relevant number. Dialling from abroad is achieved by dialling the country code 966 followed directly by the city code (i.e. without the interposition of 0).

City Codes

Riyadh
Code: 1

Jeddah
Code: 2

Dammam/Al Khobar
Code: 3

Makkah
Code: 2

Madinah
Code: 4

Yanbu
Code: 4

Jubail
Code: 3

Jizan
Code: 7

Hail
Code: 6

Abha
Code: 7

Emergency Services

Accidents
Telephone: 993

Ambulance
Telephone: 997

Fire
Telephone: 998

Police
Telephone: 999

Directory Enquiries
Telephone: 905

Telephone Maintenance
Telephone: 904

Telex Maintenance
Telephone: 930

Operator
Telephone: 900

□

Hotels and eating out, getting about

Hotels

Jeddah

Hyatt Regency – 300 rooms
P.O. Box 8483
alMadinah Road
Telephone: 6519800
Telex: 402688

Red Sea Palace – 103 rooms
P.O. Box 824
King Abdul Aziz Street
Telephone: 6428555
Telex: 401014

Meridien – 400 rooms
P.O. Box 6582
Makkah Road
Telephone: 6314000
Telex: 401327

Al Hamra Nova Park – 300 rooms
P.O. Box 3757
Palestine Road
Telephone: 6602000
Telex: 400749

Al Badr Sheraton – 563 rooms
P.O. Box 6719
Airport Road
Telephone: 6310000
Telex: 401512

Kandara Palace – 400 rooms
P.O. Box 473
Airport Road
Telephone: 6312833
Telex: 401095

Al Attas Oasis – 220 rooms
P.O. Box 1789
Off Airport Road
Telephone: 6423361
Telex: 401158

Sands
P.O. Box 7030
Al Hamra District
Telephone: 6692020
Telex: 401534

Kaki – 220 rooms
P.O. Box 2559
Off Airport Road
Telephone: 6312201
Telex: 401233

International – 80 rooms
P.O. Box 1700
King Abdul Aziz Street
Telephone: 6429022
Telex: 401116

Jeddah Palace
P.O. Box 473
Opposite Ministry of Foreign Affairs
Telephone: 6432255
Telex: 401095

Holiday Inn Opening late 1983
P.O. Box 1178
Al Hamra/Palestine Road
Telephone: 6533535
Telex: 401580

Albilad Hotel
P.O. Box 6788
Al Corniche Highway
Telephone: 6828282
Telex: 403010

Jeddah Marriott (Opened September 1983)
Palestine Road

Ramada Hotel
(Under construction)

There are a further 40 hotels in the city.

WORLD OF INFORMATION
21 GOLD STREET
SAFFRON WALDEN
ESSEX CB10 1EJ
ENGLAND
UNITED KINGDOM

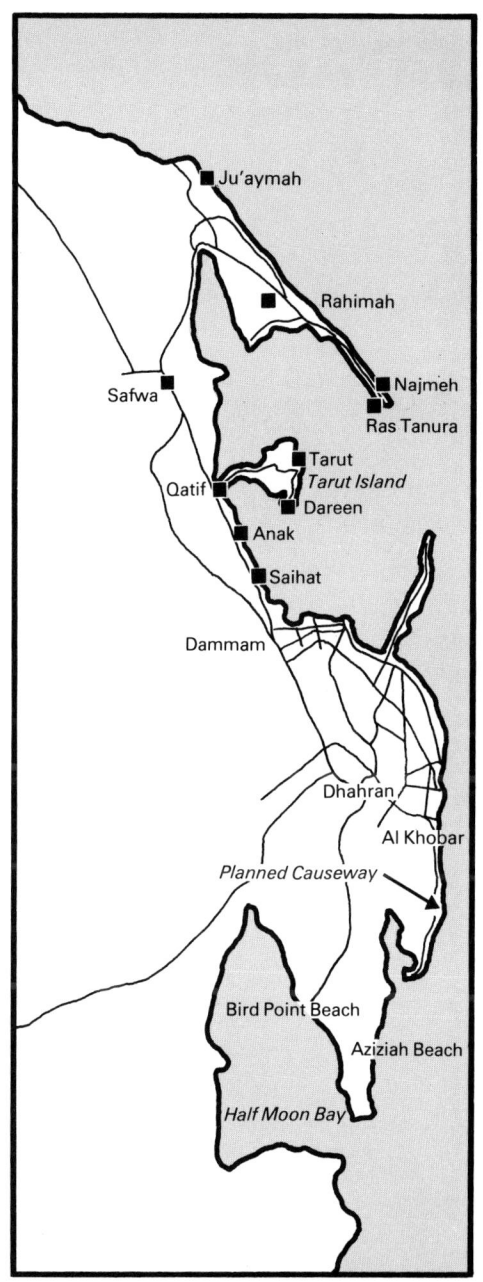

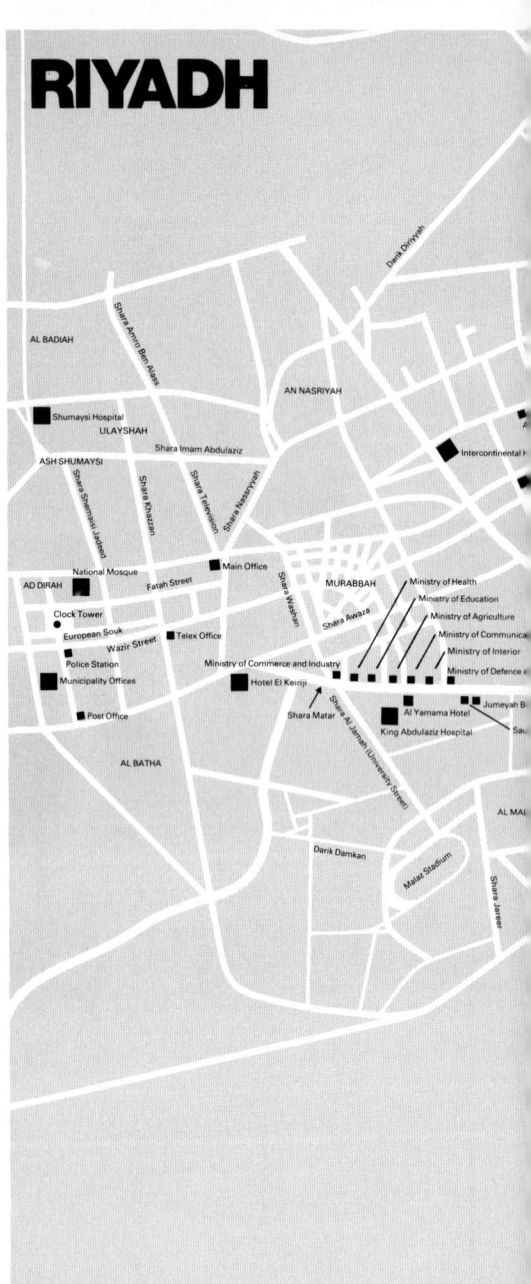

RIYADH

AL BADIAH

Shara Amro Ben Abes

AN NASRIYAH

Shumaysi Hospital
ULAYSHAH

Shara Imam Abdulaziz

ASH SHUMAYSI

Intercontinental H

Shara Shenman Jadeed

Shara Khazzan

Shara Television

Shara Nassryyah

National Mosque

Main Office

MURABBAH

Ministry of Health

AD DIRAH

Fatah Street

Shara Wadhan

Ministry of Education

Clock Tower

Shara Awara

Ministry of Agriculture

European Souk

Ministry of Communica

Wazir Street

Telex Office

Ministry of Interior

Police Station

Ministry of Commerce and Industry

Ministry of Defence e

Municipality Offices

Hotel El Keirtji

Jumeyah Bl

Post Office

Shara Matar

Al Yamama Hotel

King Abdulaziz Hospital

Sau

Shara Al Jamiah (University Street)

AL BATHA

AL MAL

Darik Damkan

Malaz Stadium

Shara Jareer

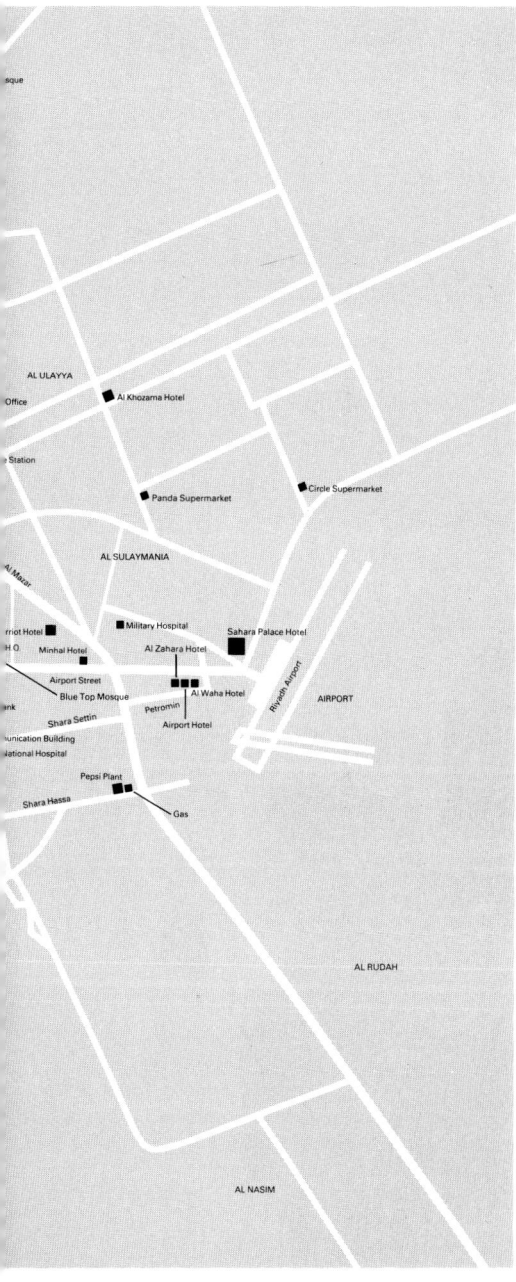

sque

AL ULAYYA

Office

Al Khozama Hotel

e Station

Panda Supermarket

Circle Supermarket

AL SULAYMANIA

Al Mazur

rriot Hotel

Military Hospital

Sahara Palace Hotel

H.O.

Minhal Hotel

Al Zahara Hotel

Airport Street

Al Waha Hotel

Blue Top Mosque

ank

Petromin

Riyadh Airport

AIRPORT

Shara Settin

Airport Hotel

unication Building

ational Hospital

Pepsi Plant

Shara Hassa

Gas

AL RUDAH

AL NASIM

51

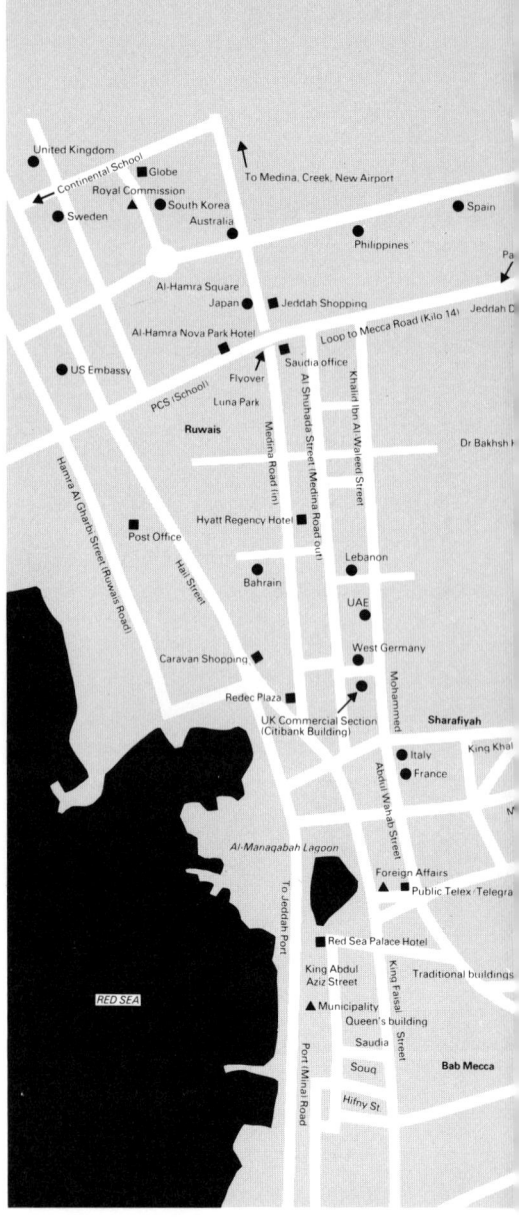

United Kingdom

Continental School

Globe

Royal Commission

Sweden

South Korea

Australia

To Medina, Creek, New Airport

Spain

Philippines

Pa

Al-Hamra Square

Japan

Jeddah Shopping

Loop to Mecca Road (Kilo 14)

Jeddah D

Al-Hamra Nova Park Hotel

US Embassy

PCS (School)

Flyover

Luna Park

Ruwais

Saudia office

Khalid Ibn Al Waleed Street

Dr Bakhsh H

Al Shuhada Street (Medina Road out)

Hamra Al Gharb Street (Ruwais Road)

Medina Road (in)

Haji Street

Post Office

Hyatt Regency Hotel

Bahrain

Lebanon

UAE

West Germany

Caravan Shopping

Redec Plaza

UK Commercial Section
(Citibank Building)

Mohammed

Sharafiyah

Italy

France

King Khal

Abdul Wahab Street

M

Al-Manaqabah Lagoon

To Jeddah Port

Foreign Affairs

Public Telex/Telegra

Red Sea Palace Hotel

King Abdul
Aziz Street

RED SEA

Municipality

Queen's building

Saudia

Souq

Hifny St.

King Faisal Street

Traditional buildings

Bab Mecca

Port (Mina) Road

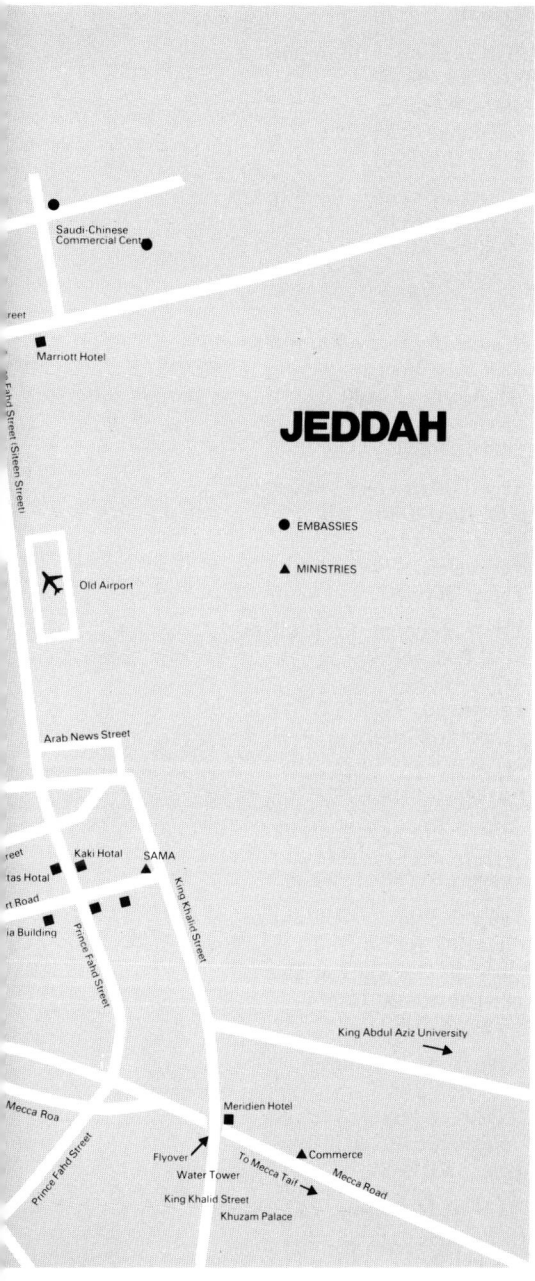

JEDDAH

● EMBASSIES

▲ MINISTRIES

Saudi-Chinese Commercial Cent

reet

Marriott Hotel

Fahd Street (Sheen Street)

Old Airport

Arab News Street

reet   Kaki Hotel   SAMA

tas Hotel

rt Road

ia Building   Prince Fahd Street

King Khalid Street

Mecca Roa

King Abdul Aziz University

Meridien Hotel

Prince Fahd Street

Flyover   To Mecca Taif   ▲ Commerce
Water Tower   Mecca Road
King Khalid Street
Khuzam Palace

Riyadh

Al Khozama – 150 rooms
P.O. Box 4148
Olaya Road
Telephone: 4654650
Telex· 200100

Intercontinental – 230 rooms
P.O. Box 3636
Maadhar Street
Telephone: 4655000
Telex: 201076

Riyadh Palace – 400 rooms
P.O. Box 2691
Off Airport Road
Telephone: 4054444
Telex: 200312

Riyadh Marriott – 403 rooms
P.O. Box 2086
Maadher Street
Telephone: 4779300
Telex: 200983

Hyatt Regency – 350 rooms
P.O. Box 18006
Airport Road
Telephone: 4771111
Telex: 202963

Minhal – 255 rooms
P.O. Box 17058
Airport Road
Telephone: 4782500
Telex: 203088

Sahari Palace – 100 rooms
P.O. Box 10574
Opposite Airport Entrance
Telephone: 4761500
Telex: 201027

Saudia – 100 rooms
P.O. Box 244
Nasseriya Street
Telephone: 4024051
Telex: 201069

Zahrat Al-Sharq – 145 rooms
P.O. Box 3616
Airport Road

Telephone: 4028216
Telex: 201017

Al Yamama – 140 rooms
P.O. Box 1210
Airport Road
Telephone: 4774039
Telex: 201056

A number of other hotels are also to be found.

Dammam, Al Khobar, Dhahran

Al Gosaibi – 190 rooms
P.O. Box 51
Al Khobar – Talal Avenue Extension
Telephone: 8942466
Telex: 670008

Carlton Al Moaibed – 248 rooms
P.O. Box 1235
Al Khobar – Between Dammam and Al Khobar
Telephone: 8575455
Telex: 670064

Meridien – 351 rooms
P.O. Box 1266
Al Khobar – Corniche Road
Telephone: 844 – 6000
Telex: 670505

Dammam Oberoi
P.O. Box 5397
Dammam – 20 mins. from Airport
Telephone: 8345555
Telex: 602071

Dhahran International
P.O. Box 428
Dhahran Airport – At Airport
Telephone: 8648555
Telex: 601226

Hotel Al-Nimran – 50 rooms
P.O. Box 340

Al Khobar
Pepsi Cola Road
Telephone: 8645618
Telex: 670

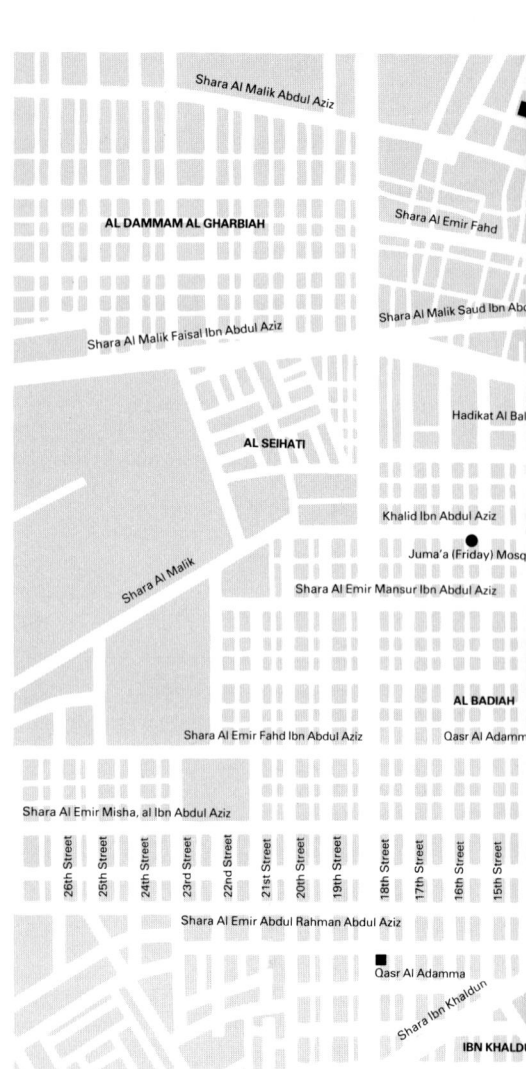

Shara Al Malik Abdul Aziz

AL DAMMAM AL GHARBIAH

Shara Al Emir Fahd

Shara Al Malik Saud Ibn Abd

Shara Al Malik Faisal Ibn Abdul Aziz

Hadikat Al Bala

AL SEIHATI

Khalid Ibn Abdul Aziz

Juma'a (Friday) Mosqu

Shara Al Malik

Shara Al Emir Mansur Ibn Abdul Aziz

AL BADIAH

Shara Al Emir Fahd Ibn Abdul Aziz

Qasr Al Adamma

Shara Al Emir Misha, al Ibn Abdul Aziz

26th Street
25th Street
24th Street
23rd Street
22nd Street
21st Street
20th Street
19th Street
18th Street
17th Street
16th Street
15th Street

Shara Al Emir Abdul Rahman Abdul Aziz

Qasr Al Adamma

Shara Ibn Khaldun

IBN KHALDU

DAMMAM

Emirate

TALAL

AL DAWASER

AMAMRAH

Dammam Baladia (Municipality)

Enterprises and General Services Company

Balhamar Hotel

Al Gosaibi Engineering Corporation

Emir Muhammad Ibn Abdul Aziz

8th Street

7th Street

6th Street

5th Street

4th Street

3rd Street

astern Provence Chamber Commerce & Industry

MUHAMMAD IBN SAUD

Al Shiha Hotel

Dammam Railway Terminal

2nd Street

AL SHAAIBAH

AL SIKKA

Gulf Flower Hotel

Postal Center

11th Street

10th Street

9th Street

12th Street

Tariq Al Dammam – Al Khobar

Sports Stadium

MEDINET AL OMAL

1st Street

adia

Al Gosaibi Engineering Corporation

57

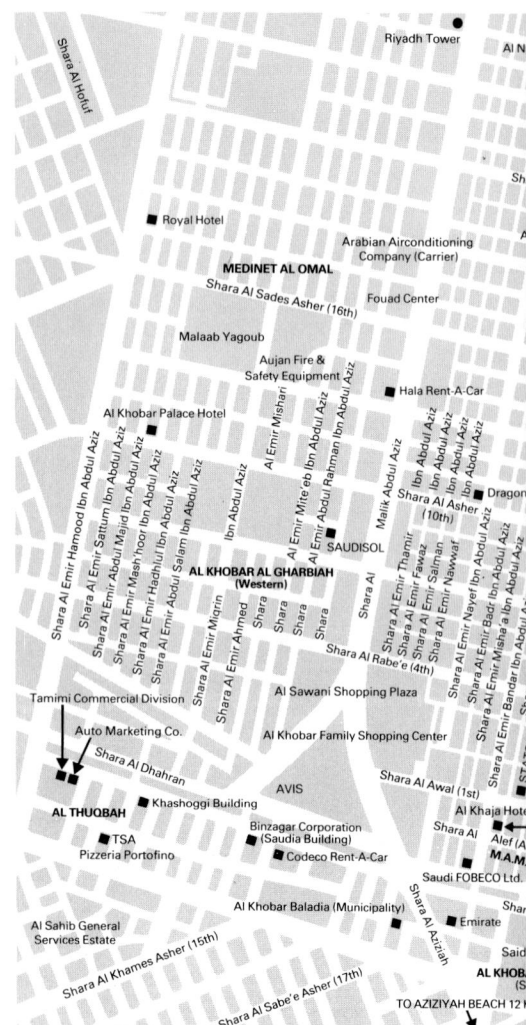

Riyadh Tower

Al Nir

Shara Al Hofuf

Shara

Royal Hotel

Arabian Airconditioning
Company (Carrier)

Al

MEDINET AL OMAL

Shara Al Sades Asher (16th)

Fouad Center

Malaab Yagoub

Aujan Fire &
Safety Equipment

Hala Rent-A-Car

Al Khobar Palace Hotel

Al Emir Mishari

Shara Al Asher
(10th)

Dragon

Al Emir Mite eb Ibn Abdul Aziz
Al Emir Abdul Rahman Ibn Abdul Aziz

Ibn Abdul Aziz

Malik Abdul Aziz

Ibn Abdul Aziz
Ibn Abdul Aziz
Ibn Abdul Aziz

Shara Al Emir Hamood Ibn Abdul Aziz
Shara Al Emir Sattum Ibn Abdul Aziz
Shara Al Emir Abdul Majid Ibn Abdul Aziz
Shara Al Emir Mash'hoor Ibn Abdul Aziz
Shara Al Emir Hadhul Ibn Abdul Aziz
Shara Al Emir Abdul Salam Ibn Abdul Aziz

SAUDISOL

AL KHOBAR AL GHARBIAH
(Western)

Shara Al Emir Miqrin

Shara Al Emir Ahmed

Shara
Shara
Shara

Shara Al

Shara Al Emir Thamir
Shara Al Emir Fawaz
Shara Al Emir Salman
Shara Al Emir Nawwaf

Shara Al Emir Nayef Ibn Abdul Aziz
Shara Al Emir Badr Ibn Abdul Aziz
Shara Al Emir Misha'a Ibn Abdul Aziz
Shara Al Emir Bandar Ibn Abdul Aziz

STATIO

Shara Al Rabe'e (4th)

Al Sawani Shopping Plaza

Tamimi Commercial Division

Auto Marketing Co.

Shara Al Dhahran

Al Khobar Family Shopping Center

Shara Al Awal (1st)

AVIS

AL THUQBAH

Khashoggi Building

Al Khaja Hote

Shara Al

Alef (A)

TSA

Pizzeria Portofino

Binzagar Corporation
(Saudia Building)

Codeco Rent-A-Car

M.A.M.

Saudi FOBECO Ltd.

Shara

Al Sahib General
Services Estate

Al Khobar Baladia (Municipality)

Emirate

Shara Al Aziziah

Said

AL KHOBA
(So

Shara Al Khames Asher (15th)

Shara Al Sabe'e Asher (17th)

TO AZIZIYAH BEACH 12 K

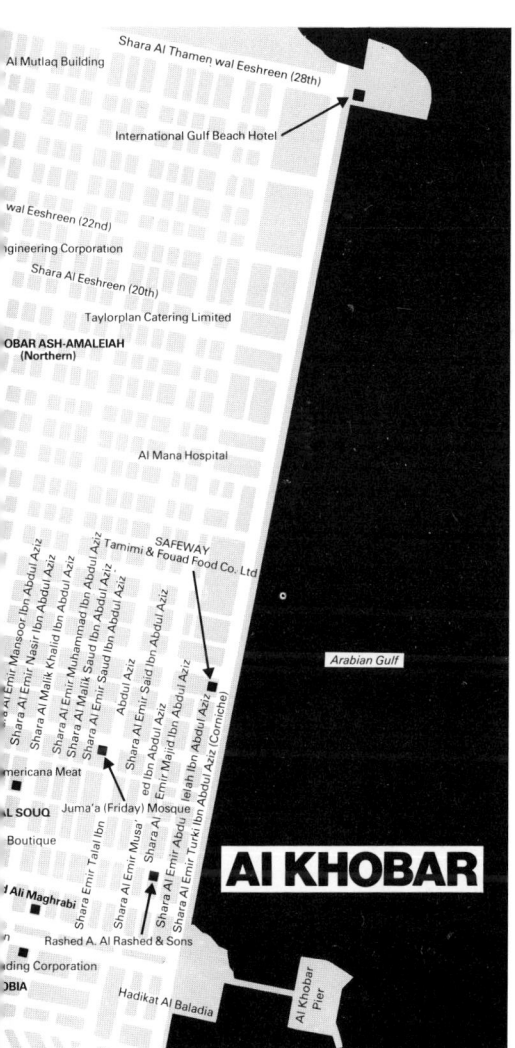

Al Mutlaq Building

Shara Al Thamen wal Eeshreen (28th)

International Gulf Beach Hotel

wal Eeshreen (22nd)

ngineering Corporation

Shara Al Eeshreen (20th)

Taylorplan Catering Limited

OBAR ASH-AMALEIAH
(Northern)

Al Mana Hospital

SAFEWAY
Tamimi & Fouad Food Co. Ltd

Arabian Gulf

Shara Al Emir Mansoor Ibn Abdul Aziz
Shara Al Emir Nasir Ibn Abdul Aziz
Shara Al Malik Khalid Ibn Abdul Aziz
Shara Al Emir Muhammad Ibn Abdul Aziz
Shara Al Malik Saud Ibn Abdul Aziz
Shara Al Emir Saud Ibn Abdul Aziz

Abdul Aziz

Shara Al Emir Saiid Ibn Abdul Aziz

ed Ibn Abdul Aziz

Emir Majid Ibn Abdul Aziz

Shara Al Emir Turki Ibn Abdul Aziz (Corniche)

mericana Meat

AL SOUQ

Boutique

d Ali Maghrabi

Shara Emir Talal Ibn

Shara Al Emir Musa'

Juma'a (Friday) Mosque

Shara Al Emir Abdul

Shara Al Emir Abdulelah Ibn Abdul Aziz

n

Rashed A. Al Rashed & Sons

ding Corporation

OBIA

Hadikat Al Baladia

Al KHOBAR

Al Khobar Pier

59

Dammam Hotel
P.O. Box 1928
Al Khobar Road
Telephone: 8329000
Telex: 601108

Balhamar Hotel
P.O. Box 2259
Dammam – City Centre
Telephone: 8320063
Telex: 601167

Al Nemer
P.O. Box 509
Dammam
Telephone: 8320641
Telex: 601149

Ramada Dhahran Palace – 205 rooms
P.O. Box 381
Dhahran – Situated in Aramco complex
Telephone: 8645606
Telex: 671259

Al Khobar Palace – 50 rooms
10th Street and Prince Hamood Street
Al Khobar
Telephone: 8648671
Telex: 670169

Royal Hotel – 100 rooms
P.O. Box 673
Al Khobar – Prince Hamood Street
Telephone: 8644076
Telex: 670056

Al Shiha Hotel
P.O. Box 1411
Dammam – King Khalid Street
Telephone: 8327877
Telex: 601449

A number of other hotels are also available in the area.

Makkah

Makkah Intercontinental – 215 rooms
P.O. Box 1496
7 Km from city centre
Telephone: 5434455
Telex: 440006

Al Fateh – 111 rooms
P.O. Box 274
City centre
Telephone: 5431353
Telex: 440083

AbdulAziz Khogeer – 286 rooms
P.O. Box 274
Ajyad Street
Telephone: 5435020
Telex: 440083

Shobra – 220 rooms
Ajyad Street
City Centre
Telephone: 5428240
Telex: 440112

Makkah – 220 rooms
P.O. Box 372
Bab Umrah
Telephone: 5747177
Telex: 440111

Ajyad Forum – 400 rooms
Opening late 1983

Jizan

Hyatt
P.O. Box 219
Telephone: 3220024
Telex: 911054

Madinah

Al Madinah Sheraton – 192 rooms
P.O. Box 1735
24 Kms from airport, outside the city and
accessible to non-Muslims
Telephone: 8230240
Telex: 470076

Qassim

Al Salman
P.O. Box 240
Telephone: 3235948
Telex: 801055

Jubail

Al Jubail International – 196 rooms
P.O. Box 1180
Near Industrial Complex
Telephone: 3610167
Telex: 670198

Rezayat Motel
P.O. Box 90
Al Khobar
4 Kms from central Jubail
Telephone: 8641066
Telex: 670006

Yanbu

Hyatt Yanbu – 179 rooms
P.O. Box 300
4 Kms from town
Telephone: 3223888
Telex: 461053

Holiday Inn – 200 rooms
P.O. Box 452
Telephone: 3223767
Telex: 461086

Taif

Massarah Intercontinental – 205 rooms
P.O. Box 827
Hawiyeh Street
Telephone: 7328333
Telex: 450010

Al Hada Sheraton – 111 rooms
P.O. Box 999
Al Hada
Telephone: 7541400
Telex: 451092

Al Aziziah Palace
P.O. Box 17
Main Square
Telephone: 7321666
Telex: 450010

Credit Cards
Most hotels accept American Express and
Diners Club in addition to a number of others.

Restaurants

Some of the best restaurants in the Kingdom are in hotels. Of special mention are the Windrose, (Al Khozama, Riyadh), Oasis (Intercontinental, Riyadh), Al Bouhaira (Red Sea Palace, Jeddah) and the Hokkaido (Japanese), Valentino (Italian), and Wong King (Chinese) (Hyatt Regency, Jeddah). Restaurants outside hotels include:

Riyadh:
Ajami (Lebanese), Movenpick Orangerie (Swiss), Ristorante Roma (Italian) and Shangri-La (Chinese)

Jeddah:
Shangri-La (Chinese), Misono (Japanese), Al Castello (Italian), Alf Laila wa Laila (Arab), and Jakarta Oriental (Indonesian).

Al Khobar:
Maxim (Lebanese/French), Silver Tower (Japanese/Chinese/Korean), Arirang (Korean).

Most, *but not all*, restaurants accept the major credit cards.

Travel Agents

Jeddah

Ace Travel
Beside Jeddah Medical Centre
Hasan bin Thabet Street
Telephone: 6533102
Telex: 403094

Air France Falcon Wings
Al Madinah Road
Telephone: 6518252

Al Attas Travel Agency
Al Madinah Road North
Telephone: 6511836
Telex: 402555

Arab Wings
Kaki Centre
Al Madinah Road
Telephone: 6674345

Areen Travel Bureau
alJohara Building
Al Madinah Road
Telephone: 6433125
Telex: 401132

Attar Travel
Jeddah Shopping Centre
Telephone: 6693464

Fahd Travels
Dhakeel Building
Palestine Square
Telephone: 6659592

Haji Abdullah Alireza & Co
King AbdulAziz Street
Telephone: 6422233
Telex: 401037

Hussein Aouieni & Co
Hail Street
Telephone: 6446475

Kanoo Travel Agency
Al Faiha Building
Al Madinah Road North
Telephone: 6534835
and
Kilo 7
Al Madinah Road (North)
Telephone: 6824432
Telex: 401039

Saudi Tourist and Travel Bureau (STTB)
Al Johara Building
Al Madinah Road South
Telephone: 6437048
Telex: 400584

Al Faisaliya Centre
King AbdulAziz Street
Telephone: 6434333

Jeddah International Market
K6, Al Madinah Road
Telephone: 6824056

Zahid Travel Agencies Co
Shohada Street
(Al Madinah Road North)
Telephone: 6515030
Telex: 403276

Riyadh

Areen Travel
At the Zahrat Al Sharq Hotel
Airport Road
Telephone: 4027685
Telex: 201699

Caravan Travel Agency
Aziziah Building
Wazir Street
Telephone: 4020022

Fahad Travel
Al Sulaimaniya
Telephone: 4480865
Telex: 201950

Falcon Wings for Travel and Tourism
Airport Road
Telephone: 4775429
Telex: 202464

Red Sea for Tourism and Aviation
Airport Road
Telephone: 4029225
Telex: 200316

Riyadh Tours and Travel Services
Airport Road
Telephone: 4028942
Telex: 201038

Saudi Tourist and Travel Bureau (STTB)
Telephone: 4013346

Saudi Travel & Tourist Agency (STATCO)
Aziziah Building
Wazir Street
Telephone: 4031752
Telex: 201125

Zahid Travel Agencies Co
Al Malaz
Telephone: 4778016
Telex: 201797

International Travel Bureau
Arabeen Street
Al Malaz
Telephone: 4788153

Saddik and Mohamed Attar Co
Al Batha Street
Telephone: 4027690

Yousef bin Ahmed Kanoo
Airport Road
Telephone: 4028942
Telex: 201038

Dammam, Al Khobar, Dhahran

Ace Travel
King Khaled Street
Al Khobar
Telephone: 8944400

Al Mojil Travel Agency
Pepsi Cola Road
Al Khobar
Telephone: 8947624
Telex: 601260

Concorde Travel
Dhahran Road
Al Khobar
Telephone: 8948857

Areen Travel Bureau
King Khaled Street
Al Khobar
Telephone: 8943005

Ewan Travel
King AbdulAziz Boulevard
Al Khobar
Telephone: 8944414
Telex: 617415

International Travel Agency
Kanoo Centre
AbdulAziz Boulevard
Al Khobar
Telephone: 8942024

Kanoo Travel Agency
King Khaled Street
Al Khobar
Telephone: 8941992
Telex: 671298

Middle East Travel and Tourism Co
Dammam
Telephone: 8324687

Wabel Travel
Dammam
Telephone: 8320090
Telex: 601433

Yusuf bin Ahmed Kanoo
Dammam
Telephone: 8323011
Telex: 601011

Zahid Travel Agency
Al Gahtani Building
Al Khobar
Telephone: 8944416
Telex: 671376

Zamil Travel Bureau
Al Khobar
Telephone: 8945634
Telex: 670132

Pan Arab Travel Agency
Dhahran Ramada Hotel
Telephone: 8945720

Jubail

Kanoo Travel Agency
Telephone: 3610369

Ras Al Khafji (Neutral Zone)

Kanoo Travel Agency
Telephone: 7660045

Yanbu

Kanoo Travel Agency
King AbdulAziz Street
Telephone: 3221087

Kurban Travel Service
Mohammed Abdul-Wahhab Street
Telex: 461021

Opening Hours
Saturday – Thursday 0800 – 1400 and 1630 – 2000

However, some agencies remain open for longer hours.

Electric Current
Can be 110 – 127V 60Hz or 220V.

Shopping – Opening Hours
Saturday – Thursday 0830 – 1330 and 1630 –
2030

Supermarkets
Many remain open from 0800 through to 2300
and in Riyadh Panda Stores remain open 24
hours.

Some stores open on Friday – especially
supermarkets and suq stores.

All stores close for prayers. (For prayer
times see the local daily press).

Car Hire, taxi services, traffic regulations, other transportation

Car Hire

Jeddah

Avis (Best Trading)
Khalid Ibn Al Waleed Street
Telephone: 6510524
Telex: 401382

Budget (Universal Car Rental Co)
Off Al Madinah Road
Telephone: 6516196
Telex: 402818

Arabian Car Rental
Meridien Hotel
Telephone: 6317274
Telex: 401119

Sahary
Mashrafa Street
North of Palestine Road
Telephone: 6602089
Telex: 402492

Abu Diyab
Sitteen Street
Telephone: 6717477

Riyadh

Avis
Salman Al Farsi Street
Al Malaz
Telephone: 4763909
Telex: 401384 (Jeddah)

Hala Rent-a-Car
Off Airport Road
Telephone: 4789986
Telex: 201969

PTS Rental Cars
Sulaymania
(Near Airport Customs)
Telephone: 4657224
Telex: 200230

Abu Diyab
Airport Road
Telephone: 4762575

Sahary
Telephone: 4650769

Shary
Near Airport
Telephone: 4766968
Telex: 203428

Dammam, Al Khobar, Dhahran

Hanco
Dammam
Telephone: 8325517
Telex: 601295

Avis
Dhahran Road
Al Khobar
Telephone: 8946085
Telex: 401384 (Jeddah)

Hala
Al Khobar
Telephone: 8941376
Telex: 670022

Codeco
Al Khobar
Telephone: 8942120
Telex: 670037

Europcar (National)
Dammam
See Hanco

Taxi Service
All taxis are orange and should now have meters
and a taxi number in evidence in addition to the

normal registration. Even though taxis have meters, and it is now an offence for a driver not to use his meter, it is best to ensure the cost of your journey in advance – as many meters appear not to work!

Fares within any city should not exceed SR10 per journey. Special care should be taken when negotiating fares to and from airports.

Saudi Limousine

The government has encouraged a number of companies to provide a limousine service both within cities and especially to and from airports. All limousines are white American air-conditioned saloons with a clearly identifiable blue and red logo marked Saudi Limousine. All fares are fixed for a specific journey and lists of these fares are prominent at the airports and are available from drivers. More expensive than taxis but more comfortable, and avoid the necessity of negotiating fares.

In Riyadh there is direct competition from Shary Limousine whose cars and logo are identical except for the logo colours which are green and red. The service from this company compares favourably with Saudi Limousine.

Buses

SAPTCO (Saudi Arabian Public Transport Company) provide a fast and efficient bus service within the three major centres. Fares within cities are SR1 per journey. Airport services are available at reasonable prices as are inter-city services between Jeddah and Riyadh, Makkah, Al Madinah, Yanbu, and Taif; and Riyadh and Qassim and the Eastern Province.

Railway

There is a railway line between Dammam and Riyadh, and two passenger services are provided daily in each direction via Hofuf. There is airconditioning and a restaurant car.

Driving

Driving is on the right. Women may not, under any circumstances, drive except within the confines of the Aramco complex at Dhahran. Valid licences from most countries will be accepted for a limited period after which a temporary local licence can be obtained. A licence valid for three years can be obtained against most clean foreign licences, after residence has been established.

Most car hire firms stipulate a minimum age of 21 and will not usually accept a licence issued within one year of the date of rental.

Driving conditions are not ideal and great care must be exercised, especially at intersections. Excessive speeds should be avoided at all times.

Car insurance is not compulsory in the country but all visitors are strongly recommended to take out at least third party cover for their own protection.

It is essential for both vehicle and private documents to be carried at all times – regular spot checks are carried out by the police.

□

Diplomatic representation

Jeddah
Embassies (Only those from Western Europe
and North America are listed here).

Austria
Telephone: 6552573

Belgium
Telephone: 6513592

Canada
Telephone: 6434900

Denmark
Telephone: 6659345

Finland
Telephone: 6515660

France
Telephone: 6515668

Germany (W)
Telephone: 6653344

Italy
Telephone: 6421451

Netherlands
Telephone: 6519024

Norway
Telephone: 6604394

Portugal
Telephone: 6674402

Spain
Telephone: 6602916

Sweden
Telephone: 6654735

Switzerland
Telephone: 6510776

United Kingdom
Telephone: 6652544 (Commercial: 6531983)

United States
Telephone: 6670080 (Commercial: 6670040)

Ministries
(Of interest to the business visitor)

Riyadh

Agriculture and Water
Telephone: 4012488

Commerce
Telephone: 4011588

Foreign Affairs
Telephone: 4771670

Industry and Electricity
Telephone: 4772722

Petroleum and Mineral Resources
Telephone: 4761133

Planning
Telephone: 4013292

□

Banks

Jeddah

Bank Al Jazira
Telephone: 6313968

Arab National
Telephone: 6422896

National Commercial
Telephone: 6443580

Riyad
Telephone: 6438383

Saudi American
Telephone: 6444111

Saudi British
Telephone: 6600944

Saudi Cairo
Telephone: 6534140

Saudi Dutch
Telephone: 6690536

Saudi French
Telephone: 6442852

Saudi Arabian Monetary Agency
Telephone: 6531122

Islamic Development Bank
Telephone: 6433994

Saudi Investment Banking Corporation
Telephone: 6604433

Courier Services

SNAS – DHL
Telephone: 6821303

SKYPAK
Telephone: 6600034

IML
Telephone: 6602000

Riyadh

Saudi Arabian Monetary Agency
Telephone: 4787400

Arab National
Telephone: 4776496

Bank Al Jazira
Telephone: 4036343

National Commercial
Telephone: 4020979

Riyadh
Telephone: 4024011

Saudi American
Telephone: 4774770

Saudi British
Telephone: 4043694

Saudi Cairo
Telephone: 4787452

Saudi Dutch
Telephone: 4015171

Saudi French
Telephone: 4760288

Saudi Investment Banking Corporation
Telephone: 4778433

United Saudi Commercial Bank
Telephone: 4774481

Courier Services

SNAS – DHL
Telephone: 4778059

SKYPAK
Telephone: 4648874

IML
Telephone: 4640424

Eastern Province

Arab National
Telephone: Al Khobar 8643488

Bank Al Jazira
Telephone: Al Khobar 8649912
            Dammam 8322709

National Commercial
Telephone: Al Khobar 8642266
           Dammam 8321566

Riyad
Telephone: Al Khobar 8642191

Saudi American
Telephone: Al Khobar 8946996

Saudi British
Telephone: Al Khobar 8649053
           Dammam 8321411

Saudi Cairo
Telephone: Al Khobar 8643940
           Dammam 8349477

Saudi Dutch
Telephone: Al Khobar 8642749
           Dammam 8323212

Saudi French
Telephone: Al Khobar 8644088
           Dammam 8320153

Saudi Investment Banking Corporation
Telephone: Al Khobar 8647506

Courier Services

SNAS – DHL
Telephone: 8643920

Calico
Telephone: 8648528

IML
Telephone: 8942466

SKYPAK
Telephone: 8340293

□

Useful information

Liquor and Drugs
The importation and possession of liquor and drugs in Saudi Arabia is strictly forbidden. A visitor found to be in possession of either on arrival in the country would face deportation and will certainly have them confiscated.

Bars and Night Clubs
There are no bars or night clubs in Saudi Arabia.

Dress
Women should always wear long dresses with long sleeves and high collars when in public areas, and men should always wear trousers and a shirt (bare chests and short shorts are offensive to many of the local population).

Tipping
A service charge of 15% is nearly always added to all hotel and restaurant bills and tipping is therefore not usually expected except for exceptional service. However, porters expect at least SR1 per item carried.

Photography
Care should always be exercised when taking photographs, especially of old buildings, as the Saudis are wary of the photographs being misused for anti-Arab propaganda. It is culturally unacceptable to photograph women and illegal to photograph any military or government installations such as ports, airports or royal palaces. Under certain circumstances permits to photograph can be obtained from the authorities.

Water
In most cities it is still recommended to boil tap water before drinking. Local and imported bottled water is readily available as is locally purified "healthy" water.

Postal Services

There are post offices in all large towns. Postal services have improved enormously in recent years but are not always reliable. Post offices are open seven days a week. Letters within a city are usually delivered the next day; between cities within 48 hours; and by air to Europe in about five days. Postal charges are not expensive.

Airline Offices

Jeddah

Saudi
Telephone: 6322222

Air France
Telephone: 6518252

Alitalia
Telephone: 6600640

British Airways
Telephone: 6693464

KLM
Telephone: 6670888

Lufthansa
Telephone: 6423324

Pan Am
Telephone: 6431151

Sabena
Telephone: 6534928

SAS
Telephone: 6693376

Swissair
Telephone: 6514000

TWA
Telephone: 6448397

Riyadh

Saudi
Telephone: 4032333

Air France
Telephone: 4776566

Alitalia
Telephone: 4023833

Austrian
Telephone: 4013962

British Airways
Telephone: 4787208

KLM
Telephone: 4771026

Lufthansa
Telephone: 4768570

SAS
Telephone: 4787212

Swissair
Telephone: 4775429

Eastern Province

Saudia
Telephone: 8944900

Air France
Telephone: 8947701

Alitalia
Telephone: 8641867

Austrian
Telephone: 8648411

British Airways
Telephone: 8942024

KLM
Telephone: 8951234

Lufthansa
Telephone: 8943800

Pan Am
Telephone: 8942977

Swissair
Telephone: 8951212

□

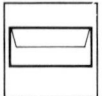

Useful business addresses

Business visitors in need of legal advice will find that in Saudi Arabia there are law firms specialising in international law or in representing the interests of foreign companies. Embassies will often be able to supply a recommended list, alternatively, the associations listed here can be of assistance in advance of a proposed visit.

Chamber of Commerce & Industry, Riyadh
Telephone: 4040044
Telex: 201054 TJARYH

Chamber of Commerce & Industry, Dammam
Telephone: 8325217, 8321134
Telex: 601089 GHURFA

Chamber of Commerce & Industry, Jeddah
Telephone: 6425659, 6424824
Telex: 401060 GHURFA

Useful Organisations and Associations

Belgium
Private Information Centre on Eastern Arabia
Heldenplein 12
Vilvoorde

France
Centre d'Information du Proche Orient
62 rue l'Homonde
Paris 75005

Germany
Nah-und Mittelost Verein
Mittelweg 151
Hamburg 13

Holland
Netherlands Institute for the Middle East
7 Prinses Beatrixlaan
P.O. Box 2085
The Hague

United Kingdom
The Middle East Association
Bury House
33 Bury Street
London S.W.1.

Arab-British Chamber of Commerce
42 Berkeley Square
London W.1.

U.S.A.
The Middle East Institute
1761 N. St., N.W.
Washington D.C. 20036

□

orbit

المدار

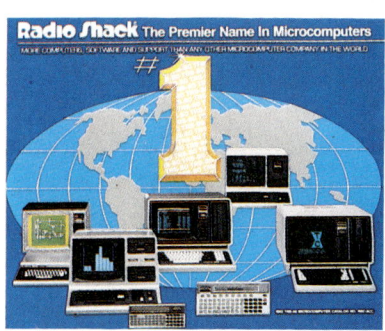

Radio Shack The Premier Name In Microcomputers

MORE COMPUTERS, SOFTWARE AND SUPPORT THAN ANY OTHER MICROCOMPUTER COMPANY IN THE WORLD

Head Office: Airport Road

Telephone: 4773146
Telex: 203511 MADAR
P.O. Box 8720 Riyadh

Branches

Riyadh: Airport Road
Telephone: 4764898

Riyadh: Olaya
Telephone: 4632887

Khobar: King Fahd Street
Telephone: 8954653

Jeddah: Palestine Street
Telephone: 6657428

Radio Shack
DEALER